KNOW YOUR
PONY

KNOW YOUR
PONY

SUSAN McBANE

WARD LOCK

RIDING SCHOOL

WARD LOCK

A WARD LOCK BOOK

First published in the UK 1992
by Ward Lock (a Cassell imprint)
Villiers House, 41/47 Strand
LONDON WC2N 5JE

Distributed in the United States
by Sterling Publishing Co., Inc.
387 Park Avenue South, New York, NY 10016-8810

Distributed in Australia
by Capricorn Link (Australia) Pty Ltd
P.O. Box 665, Lane Cove, NSW 2066

British Library Cataloguing in Publication Data

ISBN 0-7063-69785

Typeset by Chapterhouse, The Cloisters, Formby, L37 3PX

Printed and bound in Great Britain by
Mackays of Chatham PLC.

WARD LOCK RIDING SCHOOL

Know Your Pony
Understanding Your Horse
Learning to Ride
Discovering Dressage

CONTENTS

Susan McBane began riding at the age of four and has had many years' experience of riding and looking after her own and other people's horses and ponies, in widely differing circumstances.

She has been a specialist equestrian writer for 23 years and her work appears regularly in most major equestrian magazines in the United Kingdom, with some overseas contributions. She has 14 books in print.

In 1980 she founded EQUI magazine and edited this highly respected journal until, under new ownership, it ceased publication in 1985. She also helped found the Equine Behaviour Study Circle in 1978 and is still Editor-in-Chief of its six-monthly newsletter, *Equine Behaviour*.

She has a lifelong interest in the life sciences and is noted for bringing sound scientific fact to her writing, while presenting it in an easy-to-read and easily understood style. She has been described as one of Britain's leading equestrian writers, always emphasizing the practical aspects and effective principles of horse and pony management.

CHAPTER 1

THE PONY FOR YOU

When it comes to buying your own pony it doesn't matter how much or how little riding you have done because there is such a wide range of different breeds and types of pony to choose from that there is sure to be one which is suitable for you. Even very small children can easily make the step from rocking-horse to real pony as there are tiny ponies just for them. And at the other end of the scale there are large ponies or cobs which are capable of carrying teenagers or even adults.

Shetland ponies and their crosses (ponies with Shetland in them) are popular for small children. They can live out all year round and are a good starting point.

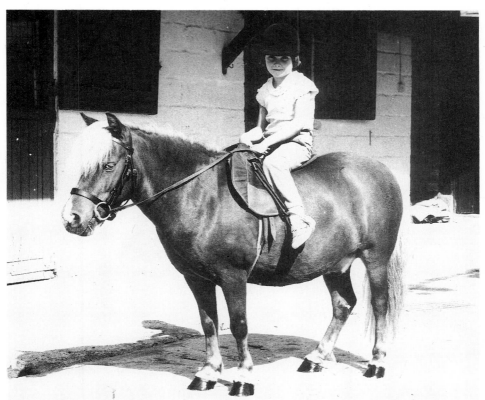

NATIVE BREEDS

Most countries have their own native breeds of pony. These breeds have existed in the wild for hundreds or even thousands of years, and have grown accustomed to the climate and conditions of their country. Britain and Ireland have several native breeds, often called Mountain and Moorland ponies because of the nature of the area that they come from.

The smaller British breeds include the little, stocky Shetland from the northern islands of Scotland, the Fell pony from Cumbria, the Welsh Mountain pony, the Dartmoor from the south-west of England and the rather special Exmoor pony – the modern Exmoor is a direct descendant of the ponies that lived in prehistoric Britain – again from the south-west. A slightly larger and very popular riding pony is the Welsh pony.

The larger British breeds, suitable for older children and teenagers, are the two types of Highland pony from Scotland (a stocky driving type of pony and a slimmer, lighter, riding type); the Dales pony from the north-east which looks more suitable for driving (having originally been a pack pony for carrying goods along trade routes) but makes a good riding pony; the Welsh cob-type pony which is about as big as the Welsh pony but stockier in build; and the New Forest pony from the New Forest, Hampshire. There is also a newish breed, the Lundy pony, which comes originally from the New Forest pony but has been bred as a separate type on the island of Lundy in the Bristol

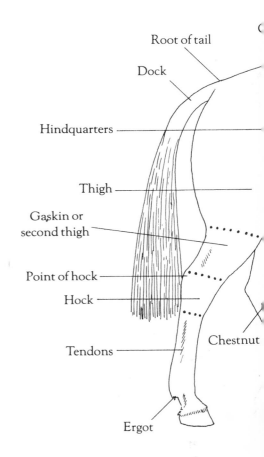

The points of a horse.

Root of tail

Dock

Hindquarters

Thigh

Gaskin or second thigh

Point of hock

Hock

Tendons

Chestnut

Ergot

Channel. It has developed characteristics of its own, and is a very attractive riding pony. The Irish Connemara is a very good riding pony, and is also used for driving.

The only British native cob is the Welsh Cob. A cob of any sort is perhaps more of a small horse than a pony. They are well-built and stocky with shortish legs for their height (up

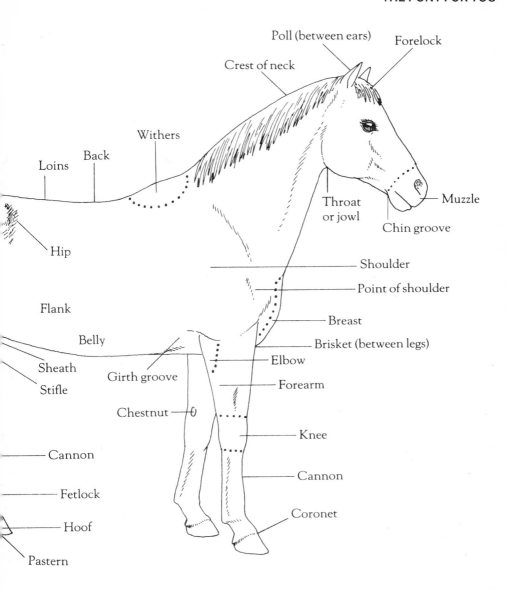

Poll (between ears)
Forelock
Crest of neck
Withers
Loins
Back
Hip
Flank
Belly
Sheath
Stifle
Girth groove
Chestnut
Cannon
Fetlock
Hoof
Pastern
Throat or jowl
Chin groove
Muzzle
Shoulder
Point of shoulder
Breast
Brisket (between legs)
Elbow
Forearm
Knee
Cannon
Coronet

to 15.2 hands high) and have strong quarters, a strong, elegant neck and attractive head which has a look more of pony about it than a horse. The Welsh Cob has both spirit and courage, as well as a showy action (particularly at the trot), and strength and stamina (which means it can work for long periods, if properly cared for, without tiring).

NON-NATIVE BREEDS

Two breeds of horse have had a great effect on most of the British native breeds, as they have on breeds of ponies and horses all over the world. These are the Arab, and the Thoroughbred which stems from it. Native ponies are very hardy; they can live outdoors (with proper land

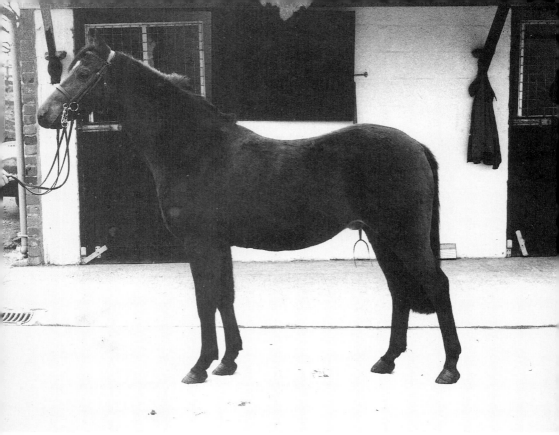

A smart, fine type of children's pony in his winter coat.

and shelter) all year round and do not need a lot of food to keep them in good condition. In the past they were crossed with Arab and Thoroughbred blood to make them more beautiful, lighter in build, and more spirited and athletic. Arabs and Thoroughbreds are not hardy, however, and breeders found that too much of their blood also reduced the hardiness of the ponies they were trying to breed, so the experiments were stopped. Some of their blood remains in today's ponies, giving them more quality (good looks and personality) without spoiling their pony character.

Arabs and Thoroughbreds are still used for crossing (breeding) with native ponies to produce various types of show pony, resulting in refined ponies that are not very hardy and need to be stabled in winter or bad weather. They have more spirited temperaments than the pure native breeds.

In many countries around the world British native breeds have been used to create new breeds. In the USA, the Pony of the Americas has been created from the Shetland crossed with the Appaloosa; in Australia, the Australian Pony has been created from the Welsh, Exmoor and Shetland breeds crossed with Arabs and Thoroughbred blood. Both breeds were developed to provide good general riding ponies for children.

One breed which is really a very small horse rather than a pony is the Caspian. Originally, this came from around the Caspian Sea and can be classed with the Arab and Thoroughbred as far as its care is concerned. Like them, it is thin-skinned and not as hardy as our natives, but has a kind nature and makes a good riding animal for children.

TYPES OF PONY

The majority of ponies, however, are of no particular breed. They are 'mongrel' ponies with many different breeds and types in them, although most will have a lot of native and some Arab and Thoroughbred blood somewhere in their ancestry. There are many excellent ponies in this category (indeed, very smart show ponies are nearly always this type of mixed-breed pony). They are often lumped together and called 'family ponies', meaning they will fit in with the family's plans, whether it be gymkhanas, hunting, Pony Club rallies, casual showing, hacking, trail-riding, or generally just having fun.

More definitive types of pony include ponies which can enter certain showing classes. Hunter ponies for example, which are smart

A sturdier type of pony, good for general riding. This coat colour and pattern is called dappled grey.

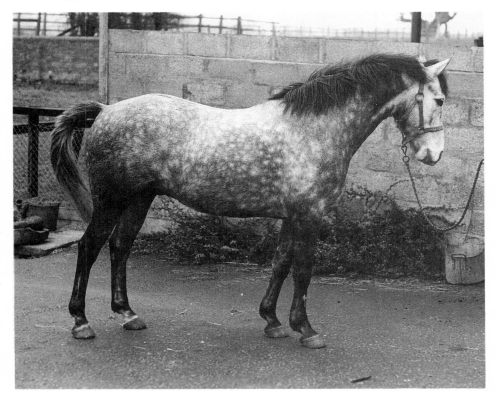

ponies, not too fine, which should be able to take a child safely out hunting. They should be able to gallop and jump, have a reliable nature and be easy to handle. Working Hunter ponies are similar, but may not be as good looking.

If you want a pony for dressage, eventing or show-jumping, it is not a type or breed you should look for, but qualities such as boldness, good action, athleticism and obedience.

COLOUR

Some show organizations specify what colours are acceptable in particular classes, and breed societies also specify acceptable colours. However, colour makes no difference at all to a pony's temperament or performance, despite many old wives' tales which say that certain colours, or even certain numbers of white socks, mean that a pony will have particular bad points. The only time that your pony may have trouble connected with colour is if he has pink skin under white areas of coat on his legs or body. Part the hair and have a look.

If a pony has pink skin under white socks, it can mean he is more likely to get a painful skin disease called mud fever if he is out on wet land a good deal. Similarly, if a pony has white patches in his coat on pink skin, he could get an almost identical disease called rain rash or rain scald in wet weather. This is because pink skin is not as tough as darker skin and does not stand up to wet weather as well.

Some ponies with much white on their noses also get skin problems if they are allergic to sunlight or some types of grass. The problem might also occur in the heels. You can buy equine sunscreens to apply to these areas, which are usually only thinly covered with hair.

If you want a pony of a particular breed or showing type it is as well to check with the organization responsible for registering such ponies as to which colours are allowed and which are not.

Chestnut ponies are reddish in colour and range from dark, chocolatey brown (called liver chestnut) to golden red, with lighter, darker or matching manes and tails.

Palomino ponies have a blonde or golden coat with silver or white manes and tails.

Piebald ponies have large patches of black and white all over.

A *skewbald* is any other colour than black, with white.

Bay ponies have brown, or sometimes dark golden, bodies with black manes and tails. Some have black legs (perhaps with white socks), when they are said to have black 'points'.

Brown can be a difficult colour to decide about. Normally the pony is brown all over. It is usually very dark, including the mane and tail, with slightly lighter mottled marks. The flanks and muzzle (nose and mouth area) may be fawn or beige.

Black ponies may be confused with very dark brown ones. The way to tell them apart is to go by the colour of the muzzle (except where there are white markings). Black ponies may be sooty black or have a steely blue tinge to their coats.

Grey ponies may have mottled marks (called dapples) or flecks in their coats. Those with dapples are called dappled grey and those with spots or flecks are called flea-bitten greys. Greys are often born dark and grow lighter with age until they are more or less white, but they are still called grey. True white ponies may have pink skin and eyes (albinos), or dark skin and either dark or blue eyes.

Roan ponies have hairs of white and any other colour sprinkled throughout their coats – white with chestnut is called strawberry roan, white with black is called blue roan.

Dun ponies have a beige coat with black mane and tail, and often a dark stripe, called an eel stripe, running down their backs.

HOW GOOD A RIDER ARE YOU?

When choosing a pony for yourself you must have a proper idea of how good a rider you are. Some people do not get ponies of their own until they are really very good riders; others start off while they are still very much beginners. Either way, you don't want a pony who is too much for you to handle or one unable to perform at your level.

Let's look at the first situation first. It's very tempting to have a glamorous, highly bred pony, rather flighty, which you'll feel good to be seen on. You need to be an

How to measure a pony

Ponies in English-speaking countries are normally measured in 'hands', a hand being 4 in (10 cm). This still applies in Britain even though we now use metric measurements for most things. Small breeds such as Shetlands are measured in inches, to be correct. Ponies are measured with a proper measuring-stick marked off in hands from the ground to their withers (the bony lump at the bottom of the neck in front of the back). Registered show ponies and those of a particular breed need a proper height certificate to ensure they are (a) in the proper class, show classes usually being divided by height of pony, and (b) not above the height allowed by the breed society where pure breeds are concerned.

If you try measuring your pony with your hands up his side you'll almost certainly find that it doesn't work out properly!

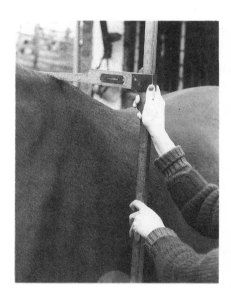

Horses and ponies are measured with a marked-off measuring stick, like this, by placing the crossbar on the highest point of the withers and reading off the height on the stick.

A very smart cob suitable for older children, teenagers or adults. Note his stocky build. His mane and forelock have been completely clipped off, known as hogging, common with cobs to make them look showier and finer. However, this does deprive a cob of the protection of his mane and forelock hair when turned out.

experienced, tactful rider to handle and be safe on a pony like this.

It doesn't take many upsets – such as being run away with or bucked off – before you won't want to ride the pony any more, or only want to ride it in a manège or indoor school, or, even worse, only in the presence of your parents or an instructor. You cannot possibly use such a pony to the full in such circumstances, or get much enjoyment out of him. It's also not fair to the pony as it means that he will not get proper exercise. If you have a pony who is too much to handle (called over-horsing yourself) you will soon be on the way to losing your nerve, becoming frightened of riding him and maybe of other ponies, too. It is also very dangerous to ride a pony you can't control properly – dangerous to yourself, the pony and other people near you. If you're out hacking, you could cause an accident on the road and be seriously injured or even killed, or cause serious accidents to other people. Over-horsing yourself is one of the most serious mistakes you can make in buying a pony.

The other situation, under-horsing yourself, is not dangerous, but it is liable to be boring if you want to progress. As you get more experience and grow bigger, you may become able to ride at a much higher standard than your pony can work at. This situation is frustrating and disappointing. You may even come to resent the pony or look down on him. However he may not be built for higher levels of work, or may not have had the training. If you don't want to ride at a high level, and particularly if you have had the pony for some time and are very fond of him, by all means keep him.

If you and your family are not sure how good you are, the best way to find out is to ask a professional instructor to give you an assessment of your riding. This can be arranged at any good riding centre if you do not have a particular instructor already. He or she will put you through your paces and ask you questions to see just how much you know and what you can do. You may feel as though you are taking an examination, but it will give you a clear idea of your ability. You can then look for a pony who has some spare capacity; that is, a pony who you like and feel comfortable on, who you can handle properly, but who is capable of working at a slightly higher level than yourself. Such a pony will help you to improve, and will probably teach you a lot, too, as you get to know each other. And you will have to ride well to keep him up to standard.

SIZE

Strictly speaking, a pony should be under 15 hands high, although true 'pony-ness' has more to do with character than height. A fair guide to the correct height for you is that when you are mounted your feet should be about level with the pony's elbow. If you get a pony that is plenty big enough for you but still within any height restrictions placed by, say, a show category or breed society, you will be able to compete on him for a few years without having to worry about selling him and getting another. If you are very tall, however, do not be tempted to get a pony that is too small for you just in order to qualify for a particular class. Most people look and feel quite silly on a pony that is too small, and it can also hold back your progress as a rider. It is far more important to have a pony with height and ability to spare than to under-horse yourself for the sake of a showing category. There are many other forms of competition if that is what you are interested in. The only exception to this is gymkhana events, when people often have smaller ponies as they are easier to vault on and off.

CHAPTER 2

LOOKING AFTER A PONY

There are various different systems for looking after a pony. The choice between them should be based on both the pony's needs and the time and money you and your family have available.

KEEPING A PONY STABLED

Under this system, the pony is kept in a stable all the time except when he is being exercised. It is the most artificial method. The pony is completely dependent on you for his every need from feeding and grooming to exercise, clothing and even fresh air. Ponies can be quite content kept this way if they are very well cared for and receive enough exercise, but many ponies are kept short of exercise and become very bored and frustrated as a result.

From your point of view, this is a very tying way to keep a pony. Activities such as feeding, mucking out and exercising, have to be done at more or less the same time every single day, and this method will take up a lot of your time. A healthy pony should have at least two hours exercise each day, and on top of that you will spend at least another two hours grooming, mucking out and bedding down,

feeding, watering, cleaning tack and rugs, and so on.

It takes a lot of experience and knowledge to operate this system, and as all the pony's food and bedding have to be bought it is also expensive, particularly if you also have to rent stabling.

KEEPING A PONY AT GRASS

This is a much more natural way to keep a pony. Most native-type ponies, and those with much native blood, are often happier this way if they have a large enough field, plenty of food and company and, most important, shelter. Many ponies are left in small fields with poor grazing, dirty water, and no real shelter from the weather and the flies.

This method can be much easier on you provided you understand that the pony will never be really clean or quite as fit for hard work as a fully stabled pony, but this may not matter. In winter, you will probably need to take hay to the field twice a day to make up for the fact that winter grass normally has little goodness in it. In addition, the pony needs checking over each day, as do his fencing, shelter and water supply.

Generally, this method is much less tying than keeping a pony stabled. As ponies often keep healthier at grass and can exercise themselves, they do not have to be ridden every day, and grass-kept ponies only need a light grooming to keep them tidy. There is no actual mucking out, although droppings must be removed from the field shelter (see p. 84) if there is one, and ideally this should be done every other day.

Grazing may have to be rented and hay, together with other feeds, bought in winter, depending on the pony's breeding and work. However, keeping a pony at grass is usually quite a lot cheaper than keeping him stabled.

COMBINED SYSTEM

On this system, ponies are kept partly stabled and partly at grass, and it is an excellent system for any pony. Often, the pony is out at night in summer and in during the day away from the sun and flies; and out during the day in winter but in at night. However, you can arrange his times in and out to suit your time and his needs.

You get the best of both worlds with this method and even though you may have to rent both stabling and grazing, the cost is probably between that of the other two methods, as you save on feed and bedding. In addition, the pony has the chance to be turned

It is best for children's ponies to be turned out to grass a good deal, even if not all the time. They love this and it is good for them to be able to eat their natural food and enjoy the freedom. You can see by the look on this pony's face how happy he is at being turned out.

Covered yards are useful and convenient for keeping horses and ponies. The animals have space to move about, and company too. Many yards can be made to open outdoors into a surfaced enclosure or field, so the ponies can come and go as they wish.

out for freedom and exercise, but can have the peace and quiet of his stable when needed.

You have to muck out once a day, and the pony needs some grooming, but exercising is not essential (and this is always very time-consuming for owners who attend school or college or who work). The pony will need to be turned out and brought in each day, and he will need hay and water when he is in. Generally, though, this method gives you and the pony the best of both worlds, and is suitable for any horse or pony.

YARDING

This system is popular in some countries. A group of ponies are kept together in a large enclosure of earth, sand or some other suitable surface

Because they are not actually in a field, the ponies usually stay cleaner than grass-kept ponies and, like stabled ponies or those on the combined system, they can be made very fit for hard work. They also have the company of other ponies, plus the space, and most ponies prefer this to being stabled.

There is no grazing or stabling to rent, but, unless the pony is at home, some rent will obviously be charged. You save nothing on feed, but bedding costs will be less. This system probably works out the same as keeping a pony on the combined system, or a little cheaper.

KEEPING A PONY AT HOME

This sounds lovely, and you have complete freedom to care for the pony exactly as you like, but you need lots of experience and time, plus the right facilities and accommodation, such as stabling, a paddock or turn-out enclosure, somewhere to store your tack and rugs, bedding and feed, and a place to pile your muck or manure where the neighbours will not complain about it or where it could create a health risk if you live near other houses. Also, most ponies are only really content when they have at least one other pony for company, so you have to find room and time for not one pony but two.

FULL LIVERY

In this method, you keep your pony at a livery yard or riding school and pay the yard owner for stabling, grazing,

material. They can exercise themselves freely (although obviously not as much as in a paddock or field). Often there is a large, open-fronted shed into which they can come and go as they wish; this really is essential if the ponies are yarded all the time and not stabled at all. They therefore have a reasonable amount of freedom so exercising is not absolutely essential. They are fed like stabled ponies, and the shed should be bedded down and the droppings removed twice daily. They can be thoroughly groomed every day, or just lightly as necessary.

feed and bedding. You may also pay for tack cleaning, grooming and exercising, depending on what services you request. In theory, you never actually have to visit your pony as the stable staff will do everything for him.

This method is ideal for people who are short of time, or who have very little experience and knowledge of looking after ponies. Expert help is on hand all the time and is well worth the cost. It can be dangerous to yourself and the pony to try to look after him entirely yourself before you have acquired the necessary skill and experience.

Although this is the most expensive way of keeping a pony, you would be well advised to have a year of full livery if you have not owned a pony before. You will learn a tremendous amount about looking after it. And you will have the chance to get to know your pony under expert supervision, particularly if you have riding lessons on your own and other ponies during that year to widen your experience.

In addition to the livery fees, you will have to pay for farriery (shoeing and foot trimming) and veterinary expenses (not only for accidents and illness but also for regular worming and vaccinations, which all ponies need). All this sounds expensive, but it is a good way to keep a pony.

PART LIVERY

In part livery, you keep your pony in a livery yard, but pay only for basic services. You may choose feeding and watering, bringing in and turning out,

mucking out and basic daily grooming. It is up to you to give the pony his ridden exercise, clean the tack, wash rugs and give a thorough grooming. This system is cheaper than full livery and a charge for stabling and grazing will be included in your fees. Your pony is getting enough care to keep him healthy, and many experienced people who find full livery rather expensive choose this system.

GRASS LIVERY

Under this system your pony lives completely at grass, and the field or yard owner should supervise him, give hay in winter or if the grass is poor due to a dry summer (for which he will charge you), and check that he is well. It is also possible to find fields to rent. You will have to check on the pony twice a day, keep him tidy, feed him and so on, as with any grass-kept pony. This alternative is quite cheap, and for those who have experience of looking after a pony, it works well as long as the facilities are good.

DO-IT-YOURSELF LIVERY

Under this system, you have to look after the pony yourself. You rent stabling and/or grazing or other turn-out facilities, as you wish, from the yard owner. However, this can be very tying; for not only do you have all the various jobs to do, you also have the time and expense of travelling to the premises twice a day, which can undoubtedly be a real nuisance, especially in winter with shorter days and unpleasant weather.

OTHER OPTIONS

There are other variations on the livery system. For example, you can get together with a group of other owners and arrange to look after each other's ponies. This cuts down on the number of trips to the yard or field, which saves both time and money. You can draw up a rota and fit in with each other. For example, you could be responsible for feeding and turning out two (or more) ponies as well as your own on, say, Monday morning if someone else does them on Monday evening so you don't have to go again, and so on. This can work well if you are all sensible, knowledgeable and, above all, reliable; if a pony seems unwell you must ring its owner, and generally co-operate with each other.

Many riding schools have a system where livery ponies are used in the school (for students and clients to ride) in exchange for a reduction in the fees. The disadvantages of this system are that the school may need your pony at weekends, which is just when you are most likely to want him yourself; also, if too many beginner or novice riders ride the pony his standard of training and schooling will go down, which will not help your riding either. If you can come to an agreement whereby the pony is used only when you don't want him, and is ridden only by proficient riders, this arrangement may suit you well.

You may be able to keep your pony with a friend's at his or her home quite cheaply in exchange for helping with the work, or simply because your pony acts as companion to theirs. This can work well provided you are sure that yours will be treated as well as theirs and not like a second-class citizen, which can sometimes happen.

You can keep your pony on someone's farm as long as the farmer understands ponies (and many do not), and the ponies are treated properly and given good accommodation.

There are various ways and systems for keeping ponies and with a little scouting around for good facilities, plus an honest assessment of the amount of time you have, how much you can afford, and how much knowledge you really have, you should be able to find something suitable.

CHAPTER 3

BUYING A PONY

Nearly everyone who rides, or even just likes ponies, dreams of having one of their own. Many parents are put off by the cost of keeping a pony, but it need not be that great. Others are put off by the fact that they don't know much about ponies, but expert help is readily available. However, it must be stressed again that no one should buy a pony of their own, if their parents or family have no experience, without learning to ride to a reasonable standard at a good riding centre.

It is important to only attend a riding school which is approved by the appropriate national governing organization for the sport. The fact that a riding school has a local licence does not mean that you will learn good horse-care and riding there. The national organization will be able to send you details of the approved centres in your area. And once you are a regular client, you will get to know other riders in your area, and build up a relationship with the owner and the instructors.

Once you are ready for a pony of your own, you and your family are strongly advised to engage an advisor or consultant, probably the owner of the school you go to. You will find that such a person charges quite a reasonable fee for advising you, finding a suitable pony and examining it, plus helping you try it out, and this is money very well spent.

You can engage a freelance advisor, someone who does not work at a particular school but teaches and advises independently. Again, someone with suitable qualifications in your area can be located through the national organization, or the Pony Club.

Your consultant will confirm that you will need to engage a vet to examine any pony you are thinking of buying. This is extremely important as a pony with any kind of disorder that might prevent his carrying out the type of work you want to do can not only prove a great disappointment or even danger, but also become expensive in vet's bills. Not all vets treat horses regularly, so try to find one whose practice includes other stables as he will be up to date in their care.

The consultant will also advise you on the necessity or otherwise of engaging a lawyer (if you want a pony with a warranty or guarantee, although not everyone bothers about this), and also on the good and bad points of dealing through an agency. Agencies put you in touch with people who have for sale a pony of the type you are looking for, and sometimes act as a go-between, but they do not normally advise on a pony's suitability.

If you want a pony of a particular breed, contact the appropriate breed society (your consultant will be able to find their address for you, or you could get it from your local reference library). Many breed societies have a register of animals for sale and wanted, and although many of them may be too young for you (you do not want a young, untrained pony but a mature, well-trained one who will look after you), some societies also have details of older animals. It's best, for a novice rider, to look for a pony at least six or seven years old and maybe a good bit older. One of this age will have acquired some common sense and can be relied on to help you. You want to look for the type of pony known as a 'patent safety pony' or 'child's first pony'. This immediately tells the owner exactly what you want as far as training, manners and temperament, are concerned. Quite elderly ponies are often suitable for this job; they are also known as 'schoolmaster' ponies because they have taught so many young people to ride.

WHERE TO BUY

This is another point to discuss with your consultant as there are several sources. As well as breed societies and agencies, you can visit reputable dealers with your consultant as here you'll see a selection of suitable ponies and can try them in an expert environment, with good facilities and knowledgeable people around you. It is not in a dealer's interests to sell you an unsuitable pony; he or she has a good reputation to keep and selling unsuitable animals can ruin his business quickly. Also, if the pony really proves unsuitable after you've had it for a while, you can often change it for another. And when the time comes for you to move on, you could sell it back to the dealer and part-exchange it for a pony with more scope.

You might like to buy your favourite riding-school pony, if he is for sale. This could be wonderful if the pony will work alone, particularly if you want to hack (ride out on the lanes and bridleways). However, some riding school ponies will only work in the company of others, which is no good for a private owner wanting to go out and about alone, or to compete in shows.

Buying from a breeder is not normally a good plan for novice riders as they usually only have young animals for sale. Private sellers can be contacted, perhaps through 'horses for sale' advertisements in local or national horse magazines, or by recommendation on the grapevine, in other words through asking around other owners.

WHERE WILL YOU KEEP HIM?

The type of pony you buy depends not only on your height and experience and the type you fancy, but also on how you are going to be able to keep him. If you can only provide a field and a shed, don't buy a thin-skinned, hot-blooded pony who cannot stand muddy ground, wind, wet and cold in winter. Instead, go for a mainly native-bred one who is tougher and won't mind cold or wet winters provided he has shelter when he wants it.

If you are going to keep the pony on the combined system, or yarded, you can buy any sort of pony. If the pony will be mainly stabled in winter (some livery stables do not permit turning out in wet weather as it damages the land) do not get one that is full of nervous energy and needs plenty of exercise, particularly if he is only going to get one hour's exercise a day because you are busy and can't afford to pay anyone else to exercise him. In this situation you will need a placid pony who won't go mad in the box.

Your consultant will know of all the decent livery stables in your area and recommend some for you to visit, perhaps visiting with you so that you can be sure the right questions are asked about services, charges and facilities. When you go, look mainly at the condition of the ponies, as that is what matters. Do they look fairly clean, not too thin or fat, interested in you and their surroundings? Are their beds, and the equipment and yard clean? Some peeling paint here and there does not matter. Just see that the people are nice and the ponies healthy and happy.

FINDING AND TRYING YOUR PONY

You'll have decided which sources to use for finding your pony, and probably your consultant has shortlisted a few for you to try. Visit the most likely-sounding one first. There is no point in travelling round several if you can find just what you want straight away.

Make an appointment that suits yourselves, the seller and your consultant (not the veterinary surgeon just yet), and go along as arranged. If when the time comes you really cannot make it, ring and tell them. This is only polite, and if you get a reputation as a 'time-waster' people with good ponies won't want you bothering them as they can easily sell them elsewhere.

Your consultant should take over once you get there, but remember that this is going to be your pony, so if you really don't like him, or really do, say so. If you do not feel comfortable with the pony, there is no point in buying him.

Note first how interested the pony is in you, and how he behaves when his present owner handles him and tacks him up. Is he co-operative or naughty? If he is in a field, is he hard to catch? If stabled, does he turn his quarters and try to kick or bite? Your consultant will expertly watch the pony being ridden and will examine his conformation (make and shape) and look for any obvious drawbacks. No pony is perfect and slight faults may not be important for your purposes; your consultant will discuss them with you. The pony will be walked about and trotted so you can all see how he moves.

When it's your turn to ride, relax! Everyone wants you to be happy, including the pony. Ponies relax with a calm rider and some tense up with a nervous one, although a good first pony won't. Ride your best, but remember that you are not taking an exam, you are getting to know a new friend. Walk about first, talking to the pony. Make a few changes of direction, a few halts, before moving into trot and doing the same. Ride a large circle, a figure-of-eight, back to

Trying out a new pony before buying is very important. Ride him in a fenced-in area first, such as this specially made outdoor school, to get the feel. You should always ride with a properly fastened chin harness on your hard hat.

walk, loose-rein walk, and so on. Then back to trot and ask for canter on both reins. If you can jump, take a small obstacle on both reins and see how keenly he jumps and how willing he is to stop after landing. Generally get the feel of him, and remember that he is wondering who you are, too, and what you want. Your consultant may well intervene and ask you to do a few movements, and ask how you like the pony's ride or feel. Do be honest. If there's anything worrying you, speak up as this is very important. If possible, watch someone else ride him in traffic to see his reaction.

If you all decide the pony is just what you want, ask if you can have a home trial. This means that you can have him for a week or so to see how you really get on. Not all sellers allow this, although dealers normally do. You may have to pay for the pony first and agree a refund if you decide against him. You will also be expected to insure him while he is with you and to pay for his transport, but your consultant and parents will deal with this.

When you have tried a pony and decided that you want him, it is very important to say that you will have him provided that he passes the vet's examination, or you may find that you are committed to buying an unsound animal.

Once you have decided that you want the pony, arrange for the vet's examination. The seller's vet cannot be used as he cannot act professionally for both of you. Although his duty is to the person paying him, if he normally treats the seller's horses he will not wish to go against their interests if there is something wrong with the pony. Look in the local services directory and ring a few vets in the pony's area. Don't get a vet from well out of the area as this will cost much more in travelling time and expenses.

The vet will let you have a certificate stating in what condition he or she found the pony on the date of the examination. Of course, if the pony becomes unsound after this date it's not the vet's fault. You must tell the vet just what you want to do with the pony so he can judge its suitability.

For instance, if you tell the vet that you want a pony for quiet hacking probably almost anything will do, but if you later try to turn it into a show-jumper and find that it cannot do the more strenuous work involved, you cannot blame the vet.

If the vet's report is favourable you can ring the seller and confirm that you will buy the pony. Your parents will probably do this and arrange payment, insurance for the pony (because once it has left the seller it is your responsibility) and transport, which your consultant will be able to advise on and maybe fix up. The seller might deliver the pony, or perhaps your livery yard can collect him. Either way, you will have to pay extra for transport unless it is included in the price (which it may well be with a dealer).

SETTLING HIM IN

If the pony is to be stabled, the stable should have been thoroughly cleaned out and completely fresh bedding put in for him. There should be a net or rack of hay and fresh water waiting for his arrival. It is a good plan to buy from the seller a couple of bales of his usual hay so it can be mixed with the hay at his new home to give his delicate digestion chance to get used to it. This also applies to any other feeds such as nuts, barley, coarse mix, or whatever he has been having. All changes in feeding must be gradual to avoid upsetting the pony. Find out about his diet and feeding routine, and if any changes are necessary introduce them over a period of two weeks or so.

If other ponies are present, he

should be stabled next to a friendly pony to give him a chance to make a new friend quickly. He has come to a competely strange place, and even if he doesn't show it he is bound to be upset and a bit worried. It may sound hard, but don't ride him for a day or two. Give him a chance to see where he is and get used to new sights, smells and sounds, together with other ponies, dogs, cats and humans. And

spend as much time with him as you can.

If he is going to a livery yard, be there when he arrives. It's important that he learns quickly that you are his owner, not the staff at the yard. Whenever you arrive at the yard go straight to him and greet him with his name, which he should learn quickly if he doesn't know it already. Let him smell you, stroke his neck, gently

Turning out for the first time

When turning the pony out into his new field for the first time, lead him right round the fencing so he can see just where the boundaries are, rather than letting him gallop off blindly. *Never* wrap the loose end of the leadrope round your hand as shown here, as if the pony takes off it could be pulled tight and you would be hurt. Show him the water supply and the field shelter if there

is one, and then turn him loose with his new friend. They will probably canter about at first, sniff each other, squeal, stamp forefeet and have a buck and a roll. This is quite normal, and enjoyable to watch. It is reassuring to know that he is settling in, and that you have done everything you reasonably can to help him.

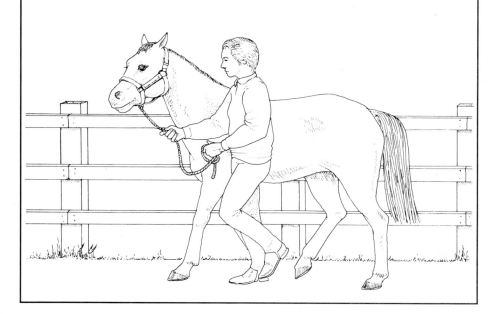

scratch his withers, and talk to him. Lead him around, groom him, turn him out and bring him in, and generally handle him, then ride him on the second or third day, depending on how he seems to have settled.

If he's going to be kept out with other ponies, it is most important that he is not just bundled into an existing herd of ponies who all know each other. It is very likely that he will be kicked, bitten and treated like an intruder. This could last for weeks or even months, making him very unhappy.

Ask the yard owner if he can be turned out with just one friendly pony at first, with the other ponies being gradually added to his herd so he is not faced with a whole gang of unfriendly, curious ponies at once. If he has a chance to make friends gradually, perhaps by riding out with the others first to get to know them, his introduction to his new life will go much more smoothly and he will settle in much more quickly.

First impressions are very important and ponies have extremely long memories. If you make sure your new pony's first impressions of you and his new home are good, he will feel at home fairly quickly, although he *will* feel strange first, just like you at a new school or in a new job. If those first impressions are bad, the pony will be miserable, may be frightened, and could become difficult to handle because he is suspicious and on the defensive all the time. Take care and this will not happen.

CHAPTER 4

CARING FOR A PONY

Many people who own ponies do so because they love riding; often they aren't so keen on the chores involved in looking after the pony and keeping him in good condition. This is a pity because working around your pony on the ground, preparing his feeds, grooming and even mucking out can help you build up a real bond of friendship. It also gives you a much better understanding of his character and state of health than just riding him can do.

FEEDING

Feeding, together with watering, is probably the most important aspect of the general care of a pony. It's true that your pony is what he eats, and that ponies have very sensitive digestive systems. Whereas dogs can

This chop – sometimes called chaff – is hay and occasionally straw, cut up small and used about a double handful in each feed, to add bulk to the feed and make the pony chew his food properly. You can buy it mixed with molasses (a form of powdered black treacle) in sacks from the feed merchant – ponies usually love the extra flavour of the molasses.

dig up mouldy old bones and eat them with no apparent ill effects, give a pony bad food and he will become ill very quickly, if he eats it at all.

Ponies developed over millions of years to live on grass, herbs and leaves. All such food is bulky and ponies have to eat large quantities in order to extract enough food value. Their digestive systems therefore developed to hold a lot of bulky, fibrous food (roughage) passing through nearly all the time. This sort of food doesn't spend long in the stomach but soon passes through to the intestines where most digestion takes place. Therefore, ponies have small stomachs for their size, and large, long intestines.

Most ponies and cobs are what are called 'good doers', which means they don't need vast amounts of food to keep weight on them and to stay in good condition. Horses need more food for their size than ponies. In the wild, ponies don't gallop and jump much, or carry riders, so they don't need to be hard and fit like a hard-working domesticated horse or pony, and the food that they graze is quite enough for them. Family ponies doing light work – hacking around, some casual showing, lessons or even half a day's hunting on Saturday – also don't need a lot of energy-producing food because they are not using up lots of energy. They can live very well on good quality hay or even just grass.

If your pony is working hard, however, such as hunting in the Christmas and Easter holidays, a hard season's showing, gymkhanas, rallies and instructional sessions and so on, he may well need a food which is more concentrated (contains more energy

and food value) than grass or hay. These feeds are called concentrates – nuts or cubes, coarse mixes, or grains you mix yourself such as barley or flaked maize. Most ponies and cobs do not need a lot of these foods, and too much can make them ill.

It is difficult to know how much and what to feed a pony, and some become too fat very quickly, which is bad for their health. The best plan is to ask your instructor, or some other qualified and experienced person, preferably who knows your pony, what to feed him, such as your vet.

Generally, he should have hay or a similar feed called hayage, which is like moist hay and is delivered in plastic-covered bales, always available

Tie up a haynet with a slip knot. Put the loose end through the loop so the pony cannot undo the knot.

in his stable. If he is too plump, use a hay or hayage with less energy value. Hayage of different brands should say on the wrapping what its energy value is; look for one with an energy value of 8·5 MJ (megajoules) of DE (digestible energy). These are measures of energy content. If the pony is working hard, or if he is living out in winter, when you need to feed him to keep out the cold, 10 MJ of DE should be right. For a pony or cob who puts weight on easily, a product with only about 7 MJ of DE will be right.

Ordinary hay won't have this sort of information unless you buy it from a really good feed merchant who has had it tested. Just ask for clean, good quality meadow-type hay. Do not buy seed hay, ryegrass hay, timothy hay, clover hay, or mixture hay or racehorse hay, lucerne, alfalfa or sainfoin hay, as they are too rich for a pony. Mixture hay is all right for hard-working ponies or those out in winter, however.

If your pony always has hay available when stabled he will probably not need any concentrates. However, if he is in a yard where other ponies are getting short feeds (feeds in a bucket or manger), he may feel left out if he gets nothing. In this case, you can give him a 'false' feed – one which will satisfy him without over-feeding him. Buy some bulky food such as molassed chop or chaff (hay and straw cut up small and coated in molasses) and mix with it something juicy such as soaked sugarbeet pulp or thinly sliced carrots (sliced lengthways so there is less chance of chunks sticking in the pony's throat). If you give him two double handfuls of chaff (more for a large pony), and about 1 kg (2¼ lb) of carrots or a double handful of soaked pulp, all mixed up, this will keep him happy.

Sugarbeet pulp is a very useful feed for ponies but it *must* be soaked well in cold water before use, otherwise it can swell up in the pony's throat, stomach or intestines, which may kill him. It comes in flakes or hard cubes, often

Soaked sugar beet pulp is a useful, juicy feed for ponies and most of them like it; it must be soaked for 24 hours in twice its own volume of cold water before being mixed with the feed. On the right, sugar beet in cube form is shown and on the left, the same amount after proper soaking. You can see how much the beet swells.

mixed with molasses, and is dark grey in colour. Take one double handful of dry pulp and put it in the bottom of an ordinary stable bucket. Fill the bucket almost to the top with cold water and leave it to soak for 24 hours, then it will be ready. If you want it ready for use for the tea-time feed on Sunday, put it to soak at tea-time on Saturday.

You should buy concentrate feeds in the form of pony cubes or nuts (which you can tell from sugarbeet cubes because they are usually greenish or beige in colour) and coarse mixes. Coarse mixes contain several different ingredients such as barley, maize, little cubes, locust beans and so on, all mixed together in a sack. Ponies usually love them even more than nuts. For an inexperienced owner, cubes or coarse mixes are the safest feeds to buy, because they are available at the right energy level (described earlier), so you don't have to worry about adding anything else (other than carrots or sugarbeet pulp if you wish). Such feeds are described as correctly balanced, which means that they contain the right amounts of the different foods the pony needs to keep him well. Although vitamins and minerals, which are needed in small but exact amounts, can be bought as supplements, they are already added in the right amounts to nuts and coarse mixes. You are not advised to try to create your own feed mixes as this requires expert knowledge.

Bran has been a popular feed for years, but too much can cause bone disease and it's also very expensive for the feed value it contains. It is rather tasteless and is not a valuable pony feed, despite what you may hear. You may hear that you should feed your pony a 'bran mash' before a rest day each week, but this is old fashioned advice, bran mashes are unnecessary, and can be harmful. If the pony is turned out every day, and is receiving small quantities of concentrates, he will not need anything else. If he is stabled because of an injury, feed him hay, water and maybe false feeds, and he will be fine.

If you do want to give concentrates, take your instructor's advice. A pony's digestive system needs time to get used to a new type of feed, so start off with very small amounts – no more than 250 g (½ lb) per day at first, maybe even less – split between his short feeds, gradually building up to what your instructor thinks is right for your pony. Don't reduce the hay or hayage, however, as these are very important to stop your pony feeling hungry and chewing his stable or bedding, for entertaining him, and providing food value.

WATER

Water is absolutely essential for your pony and he should always have clean, fresh water in his stable or field. Don't rely on a dirty-looking pond or stream, which may be polluted even if it doesn't look it. Make sure he has a clean supply from the mains, provided in a trough or other container.

RULES OF FEEDING

ʊ *Cleanliness* All feed and water containers used in the stable or field should be scrubbed out with clean water daily. This can't be done with water troughs, of course, but they should be emptied, cleaned, rinsed down and refilled every few weeks.

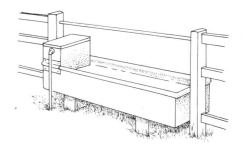

A water trough can be made to serve two fields by fitting it into the fence.

ʊ *Feed little and often* This imitates the way ponies eat in nature. Make sure your pony always has hay or hayage, plus water, when stabled. If you feed concentrates, remember to split the total amount into two or more feeds over the 24 hours. Small ponies should have no more than 1 kg (2¼ lb) total weight in one short manger feed, larger ponies no more than 1·5 kg (3¼ lb).

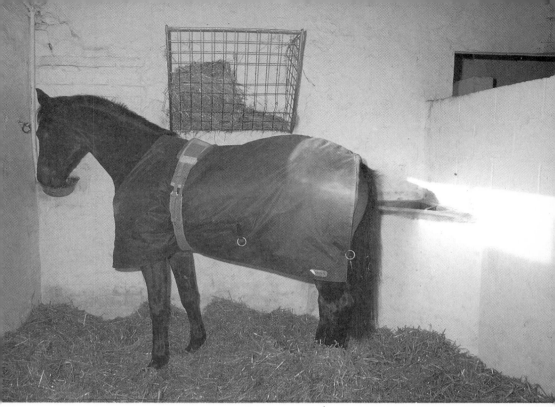

A light, airy stable with an automatic drinking bowl on the left and a corner manger on the right, bricked in underneath so that the pony cannot get his head or legs caught underneath it. The hayrack in the middle of the wall is a good type, but corner styles are safer and the pony cannot knock his head on them. The bedding is clean straw, but it should be banked up round the sides of the box for extra warmth, comfort and safety. The rug being worn is a modern, shaped type with leg straps and should not need the roller the pony is wearing. In fact, the roller will prevent the rug from falling in the correct position and the pony will not be so comfortable as he would be without it.

℧ *Make no sudden changes in feeding*
When starting on a new sort of feed, give very small amounts, even just a handful, mixed with familiar feed, and increase it very gradually to give his digestive system a chance to get used to the new feed, otherwise he could become ill. Don't feed a weekly bran mash, particularly if your pony doesn't normally get bran, as this represents a sudden change. Always give the same things in each feed – don't, for example, feed cubes for breakfast, coarse mix for lunch, chop and beet pulp for tea – this is bad for the pony. You can change the amounts up and down safely but not the ingredients.

Ω *Always feed clean, good quality feeds*
Feed should never be dusty, mouldy or sour- or musty-smelling. Check hay particularly. If it is dusty or has white, green or black patches of mould on it, or if it smells musty or sour, don't accept it. Don't be afraid to complain, or you will get bad hay palmed off on you again. And don't accept the excuse 'it's all right for ponies'.

ʊ *Feed something succulent (juicy) each day* This imitates the pony's natural food, grass. Ponies need juicy food, particularly when grass is scarce or when they are not turned out much. About 2 kg (4½ lb) of carrots, thinly sliced or grated, can be added to the daily feeds on top of the concentrate allowance, or mixed with a false feed. Sugarbeet pulp also counts as a succulent feed. If your pony likes turnips, swedes or mangolds, leave a whole one in his manger for him to scrunch on overnight.

ʊ *Feed according to work, condition and the weather* The ponies needing most food are those working hard, those in poor condition (thin), or those out in winter. Although you won't go wrong, normally, by giving your pony plenty of hay, you must be very careful with concentrates, and always take advice. It's safer to slightly underfeed than overfeed, and if you are not sure how much to give don't give any concentrates at all. If your pony expects a short feed give a false feed instead. If your pony's work is going to be cut down, cut down his concentrates first (the day before): if his work is going to increase, increase his concentrates on the day.

ʊ *Never work hard on a full stomach* If your pony is grass-kept and eats most of the time, you can ride him straight from the field, but just walk or trot slowly for the first half-hour to give the grass chance to go down. Stabled ponies should have their haynets taken away an hour before exercise. They should not be worked for at least an hour after they have finished a short feed.

ʊ *Water before feeding* Most ponies have water always with them so this is less important than in the past when they were led out to drink at a trough. If ponies who always have water with them drink during or after feeding, this is quite safe as they will not drink much. If ponies don't have water always available, offer water before a feed. If they don't want it, feed them and don't give water for an hour afterwards, otherwise they could be ill.

ʊ *Keep to the same feed times each day* Ponies who have hay always with them can put up with manger feeds being a bit late or early, but generally their digestions work best on a proper routine. Also, they will expect feeds at regular times and can become upset if these are missed. If you are going to a day-long show or hunting, take the pony's lunch, or at least let him graze at the appropriate time, otherwise he will feel uncomfortably hungry and just might be ill later.

ʊ *Don't give vitamin and mineral supplements unless advised by an expert* The vet will tell you if your pony needs a supplement. Too many vitamins and minerals can make your pony ill. Don't be tempted by advertisements or by friends who recommend a supplement.

HOW MUCH IS ENOUGH?

As a rough guide, a small pony of about 12 hands might need about 3 kg

(6½ lb) of hay a day; a larger one of about 14·3 hands about 5·5 kg (12 lb). With hay it's better to give too much as the pony will leave what he doesn't need. You can use it again, so it won't be wasted.

With concentrates, on the other hand, it is important to give exactly the right amount. Small ponies rarely need concentrates. In winter, or if stabled and working hard, they might need 500 g–1 kg (18 oz–2¼ lb) a day, plus succulents. A pony of 14·3 hands with a good deal of Arab or Thoroughbred blood, working hard and stabled or out a lot in winter could need roughly 3 kg (6½ lb) of concentrates a day split into two feeds.

Don't guess at weights. Buy a hay-weigher (a simple hand-held, spring type is fine) from a feed merchant or good tack store, and hook your haynet on to it, reading off the weight from the scale. Ordinary kitchen scales can be used for weighing concentrates and succulent feeds like carrots or apples (which should always be eating apples, baking apples can cause colic – feed them in the same amounts as carrots).

JUDGING BODY CONDITION

You need an experienced eye to tell if your pony is too fat or thin. You should just be able to feel his ribs along his side under his skin. If you can't feel his ribs under his skin, he's too fat: if you can actually see them, he's too thin. If he has a woolly coat in winter, push your fingers through the hair and feel for his ribs.

BEDDING

Ponies need good beds in their stables and field shelters to encourage them to lie down and rest, to keep them warm and comfortable, and to protect them from possible bruising on the floor. Stabled ponies cannot get away from their beds, so remember that they must be kept as clean, thick and dry as is reasonably possible. Badly kept beds soon start to smell, and give off fumes which badly affect the pony's lungs and breathing and also the horn of his hooves.

Materials

The most popular and common bedding materials are straw and wood shavings. Less commonly used are shredded paper (an excellent bedding material), sawdust (very good) and peat (absolutely terrible). You can get bedding material from most agricultural suppliers or feed merchants. Alternatively, you can find a local supplier in horse magazines or farming journals.

Manure

Manure must be disposed of effectively, particularly in stables near houses, as it can smell and attract flies. A livery yard will have suitable arrangements for this; they will probably sell it to a contractor or nursery for growing mushrooms, vegetables or flowers. Cleaning out the pony's stable is called mucking out; putting down his bed, or adding new material, is called bedding down. Tidying his bed is called setting fair; removing droppings and the very dirtiest, wettest bedding material is called skipping or skepping out.

Different ways of managing beds

There are three methods of keeping your pony's bed in good order.

Full mucking out and bedding down
All the droppings and dirtiest bedding are removed and the half-dirty material is saved to use as the bottom layer of the new bed. The floor is swept and scraped clear of all stubborn dirt, rinsed down if possible and the bed redone adding new material on top. It is hard work and takes half an hour per stable if you're used to it – much longer if you're not! It is the most thorough system, though, and does keep the stable healthier, cleaner and free from smells.

A completely different system is *deep litter*. Only the droppings are taken out, and fresh bedding is put down. Eventually the bed builds up into a thick cushion on the stable floor. If the stable is properly drained and airy it can work well. The best material for this system is straw. You must remove droppings at least three times a day for a stabled pony, and preferably more often, so it's not suitable for anyone who cannot manage this. The pony will trample them into the bed otherwise and make the bed very hard to keep in good order.

Another method is *semi-deep litter*, half way between full deep litter and mucking out. You remove the droppings and the worst of the dirty bedding each day, bring in clean bedding from the sides of the box and add new material on top. This method is useful for people at school or work during the week, who often only muck out fully at weekends when there's more time.

How to muck out and bed down a straw bed

The tools needed for this job are illustrated in the photograph. First pick up all the obvious droppings on a shovel, using your foot to push them on to the shovel, or, if using shavings, your hands in rubber gloves if you find this difficult. Put them in the wheelbarrow. Place the clean material in the cleanest corner of the box and separate, with the fork, all the half-dirty straw and pile it in a different corner. You'll be left with the dirtiest straw and any droppings you missed earlier. Shovel this all out into the wheelbarrow and wheel it to the muck heap.

Now thoroughly sweep the floor, scraping off stubborn dirt with the back of the shovel. If possible, rinse down the floor with a hosepipe or bucket of water, and leave the floor to air and dry while the pony is out at exercise. You can move your two piles of straw to other corners and sweep where they were so you have a clean floor area. Sweepings, too, go into the barrow and on to the muck heap.

To bed down, take the pile of half-dirty straw and lay it evenly over the floor using the fork. Next, do the same with the clean straw that you saved, spreading it evenly on top. Lastly, take the new material and spread that over the top. Also place plenty all round the walls (called banking up) to act as a cushion when the pony lies down. Make sure there are no lumps of straw, or binder twine or even wire from the bales left in the bedding as these are dangerous.

Shavings beds are prepared in the same way, although many people keep shavings on a semi-deep litter system.

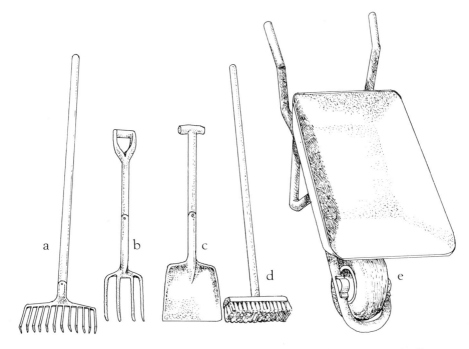

Mucking out tools. (a) shavings rake, (b) four-tine fork, (c) shovel, (d) broom, (e) wheelbarrow.

The secret of a successful bed with any material is to remove all the droppings as often as you can, otherwise the bed will soon look like an indoor muck heap.

HOW MUCH BEDDING SHOULD YOU USE?

Many people keep the pony's bed too thin. Thin beds and so-called day beds (very thin beds) are useless. They don't keep the pony warm or protect him when he lies down, they don't encourage him to lie down, and they get dirty very quickly. Use the fork as a guide and stick it down through the material. It should sink in up to the bottom of the handle, the bedding covering the prongs of the fork, and it should feel like a firm, cushioning mattress under your feet. It is *not*

extravagant or wasteful to keep a good, thick bed. It is correct management and helps keep your pony in good comfortable condition. Also, don't leave a bare patch behind the door. Stabled ponies spend a lot of time standing here looking out and it's better for them to have something soft to stand on. It also helps to prevent floor-level draughts.

GROOMING

Stabled ponies are normally fully groomed every day as they do not get rained on (which cleans the coat). As they are normally working harder than grass-kept ponies their skins (which through sweating help get rid of certain natural poisons formed during hard work) need to be in tip-top condition to cope with the work

Grooming kit:

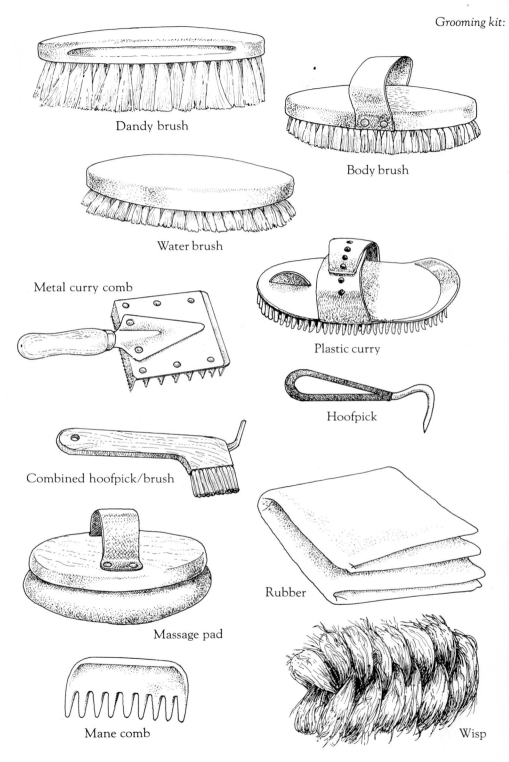

Dandy brush

Body brush

Water brush

Metal curry comb

Plastic curry

Hoofpick

Combined hoofpick/brush

Rubber

Massage pad

Mane comb

Wisp

To pull the mane, run a mane comb up the hair so you are left holding the longest hairs, and, pressing your thumb against the comb, pull out just a few hairs (six is plenty) at a time from the roots with a quick tug. Don't try to do the whole mane at once, as this will make the pony's neck sore and he may resent the operation next time.

and extra feed they often have. The skin naturally flakes off as it grows older, forming the dandruff you see in an ungroomed pony's coat, so this, together with the natural grease

which forms in the coat, has to be removed. Outdoor ponies, however, are not groomed so thoroughly as they do get wet, and they also need grease in their coats to help protect them from the cold. Dirty skin can encourage skin disease and lice, so you should always keep an eye on even outdoor ponies and not let them become too dirty.

Full grooming, a basic routine

First take the dandy brush and brush off (not *too* hard) all dried mud and dried-on muck ('stable stains'). Using the dandy brush, the body brush or your fingers, carefully remove bits of bedding from the mane, tail and forelock. Also undo any tangles, taking care not to break or pull out the hair any more than is unavoidable, although it is natural for some hair to be shed all the time.

Now take the hoof pick and pick out all droppings and/or mud from the

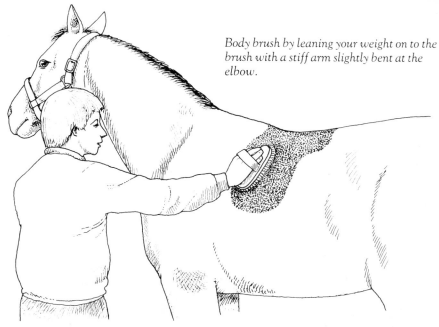

Body brush by leaning your weight on to the brush with a stiff arm slightly bent at the elbow.

feet, using the method shown in the picture. Don't let it all fall into the bed but into your muck skip (a dustbin lid makes a good skip).

Take the body brush and hold it as shown in the picture. Keeping your arm stiff but relaxed, and with a slightly bent elbow, brush the pony firmly all over. Use long, sweeping strokes where you can, about six on one spot being enough. After every two or three strokes scrape the brush over the metal curry comb to clean the bristles. Every now and then, tap the curry comb on its side near the door or outside if the door is open (having tied up the pony so he can't nip out).

When doing the head and legs, or any boney parts, be careful not to

To pick out the feet, hold the hoof as shown and work from the heels to the toes so that no dirt or grit is pushed under the loosest parts of the shoe, the heels.

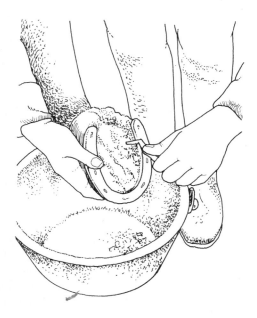

knock the pony with the brush, because if you hurt him he could become difficult to groom in future. Body brush all over the pony, taking care not to forget the parts many people do forget, namely under the forelock, inside the ears, under the mane, under the jaw, under the belly and between and inside the legs, also under the tail between the buttocks, and finally behind the pasterns.

Still using the body brush, brush out the forelock from the roots, getting right underneath it. Push the mane over to the wrong side of the neck. Starting behind the ears, brush it out from the roots a lock at a time; bring it back over to the normal side of the neck as you go.

To do the tail, first brush the hair on the dock getting right down to the roots, then hold the dock at the end with your hand right round the long hairs, and hold the dock up towards you, level to the ground. Letting down a lock at a time, brush the tail right down to the roots, but start at the *ends* of the hairs so as not to create tangles as you go. Gradually let down all the hair as you brush.

Now take your two sponges, one for the eyes, nostrils and lips and the other for the sheath (or udder in a mare) and under the dock – and never mix them up. Dip the sponge in a bucket of clean water and squeeze it out as hard as you can so it is damp, and sponge clean the parts just mentioned. In winter, dry them with an old towel.

If you have a water brush, dip the tips of the bristles in the water (never use the pony's drinking water) and shake off the excess water with a firm downward shake. Brush the mane hair right from the roots on the crest of the neck, to flatten it down, and do the same with the tail hair on the dock. Finally you can give the pony a final dusting down with the stable rubber and you've finished.

Some people oil the hooves, but most hoof oils don't do any good and simply pick up bits. Don't bother with hoof dressings unless advised to use them by your farrier or vet.

When brushing, always work back and down so as not to brush dirt over parts already done. It's not necessary to use your left arm for the pony's left side and vice versa. Change arms if you get tired, as otherwise you won't do a proper job. This routine will take

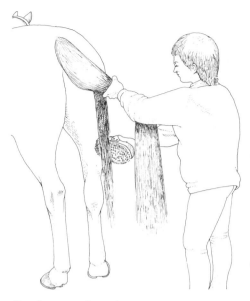

Brushing out the tail.

It does no harm at all to rinse your pony down to clean him, provided he is not hot when you do it and that you dry him off quickly and properly afterwards. It's best to get a friend to hold your pony, if possible, so he or she can calm and control the pony if something should frighten him.

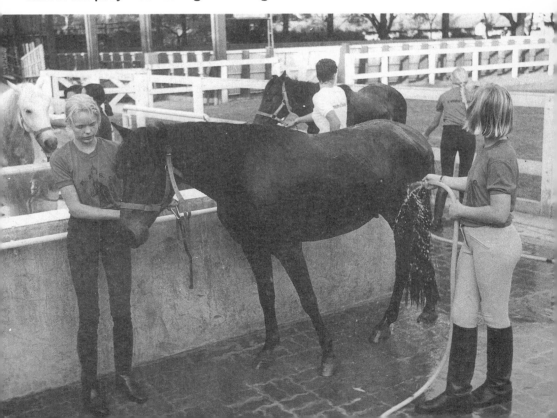

Different types of clip.

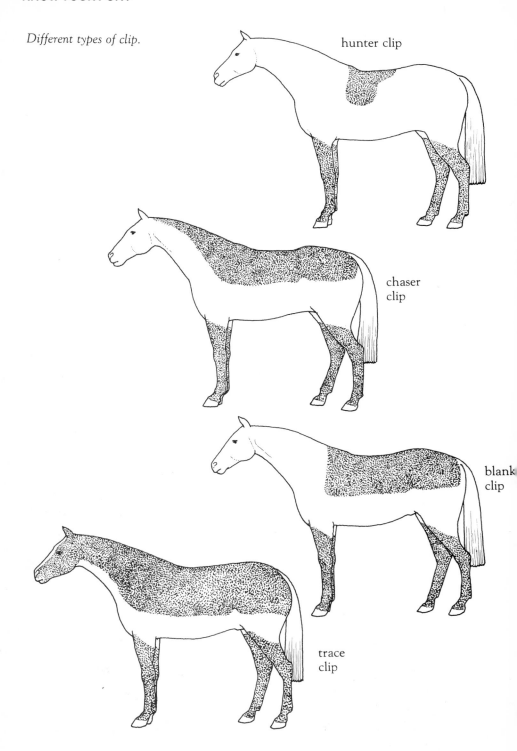

hunter clip

chaser clip

blank clip

trace clip

you half an hour if you're fit, longer if you're not. You'll get hot and tired if you work properly, but as you improve it will get easier. It's excellent for warming yourself up on a cold day.

CLIPPING AND TRIMMING

Ponies' coats often grow woolly and untidy if they are not clipped and trimmed, and you should arrange to have this done by an expert.

Native-type ponies can grow really thick, furry coats in winter and if they are working at all hard they will have to have their coat clipped, otherwise they will sweat too much when working and lose weight, and they will also get chilled as they start to cool down. They will cool down before their thick coat has dried, and feel colder than ever.

The pictures show different types of clip, take advice as to which is suitable for your pony. Clipping is a skilled job and you will probably have to pay someone to clip your pony. Before clipping, your pony must be clean and dry, otherwise the clipper blades will pull and hurt him. The clipper is an electric machine with carefully adjusted blades. It makes a buzzing noise which some ponies don't like. In fact, some are really frightened of it. If your pony is frightened, it may be that you cannot have him clipped, or that he will have to be tranquillized by the vet first. Take your instructor's or consultant's advice on this.

If you have never seen a pony being clipped, you will probably find it fascinating to watch the hair peel off and the pony change colour before your very eyes. All ponies are lighter

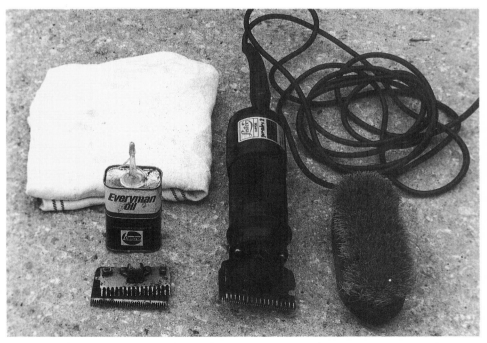

Clipping equipment: left, a stable rubber, oil and blades. The clipper is in the middle and, on the right, a brush to finish off.

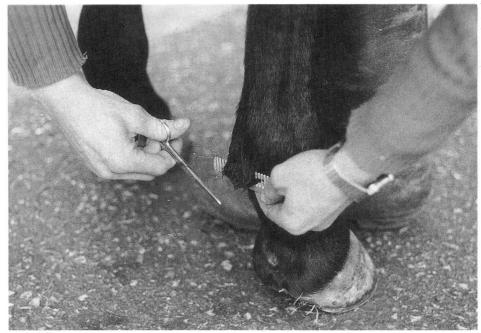

To trim the fetlocks, comb the hair up the wrong way and snip off the hairs which come out through the comb, leaving a little tuft at the bottom of the fetlock for water to drip off.

(except greys) under their top coats. Blacks go blue or charcoal grey, and chestnuts go beige. Clipping is a long process and it's a good idea to hang up a haynet for your pony to nibble at. Also have a rug handy to put over his quarters as clipping progresses, so he doesn't get chilly and fidget.

After clipping, rub the pony over with a stable rubber wrung out in hot water. This removes excess grease next to the skin together with short, prickly bits of hair left in the coat. Body brush him over quickly and rug him up. If you wait until the pony's winter coat has fully grown (set), you shouldn't need to have him clipped again that winter. His winter coat will start coming out in early spring, getting up your nose, down your

throat and in your clothes. It takes several weeks for it to come out completely and reveal his new, short summer coat underneath. The summer coat, in turn, starts noticeably coming out in late summer and, likewise, takes several weeks to set.

Trimming, as opposed to clippping, involves removing excess hair from mane, tail, under the jaw, from the outside edges and base of the ears (never remove hair from the inside of the ears) and from the lower legs. A trimmed but unclipped pony can look quite neat enough for most people. Like clipping, it takes practice and the person who clips your pony can probably trim him, too. Manes can be thinned out and shortened; tails can be shortened to about hock level for winter so they do not gather too much mud. Whiskers can be pulled or trimmed with scissors and comb from under the jaw, and trimmed with scissors from the edges and base of the ears. Pastern or heel hair can be trimmed again with scissors and comb, which gives a smoother finish than clippers on the legs. The top of the tail (dock) can be tapered in appearance by having the hair pulled from the side although this, like having the mane done, should be done over a period of a few days as it can otherwise make the pony very sore. However, for a pony who is out a good deal, it is kinder not to trim (pull) the tail as he needs the hair for protection. When special occasions arise he can have his tail plaited along with his mane, if you wish. Ponies of a registered breed, however, have to be shown 'natural', untrimmed as far as mane and tail go, and look better that way anyway.

Ponies grow coarse, longish whiskers around their muzzles which many people clip off. However, these whiskers are very important to the pony for feeling his food and other things that he investigates with his nose and lips. They act as 'antennae' or feelers, especially when sorting out grass, or in the dark, and should really be left. It is certainly unkind and quite unnecessary to remove them. People who say that ponies look messy with these whiskers left on are more concerned with fashion than with their pony's well-being. It is a sign of a kind, caring owner to leave them on.

CHAPTER 5

HANDLING AND STABLE ROUTINES

HANDLING YOUR PONY

It is very important that you learn to handle a pony correctly as bad handling can completely ruin a well-mannered, sweet-natured pony. Ponies are big, strong animals, but they are also easily frightened and you can be hurt if you do things wrong.

You should cultivate a quiet, confident manner when handling ponies. If you are timid or nervous they will sense it and could react in one of two ways. They, too, might become timid and nervous, sensing that there is something around to be afraid of. They may not realize that you are nervous of them. On the

To turn your pony, walk on the outside of him – like this – and push him away from you on the bend. This way he'll keep his balance and won't tread on you.

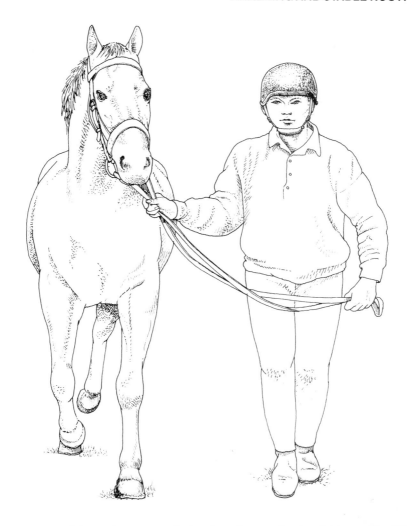

To lead a pony in hand, bring the reins over his head, walk or run level with his shoulder. Wear your hard hat, strong shoes or boots and gloves, to protect yourself should the pony trip. Hold the reins a little way down from the bit and hold up the loose end in your other hand. Never link your arm through the loop of the reins when leading, or wrap the reins round your hand or wrist, as you could be dragged if your pony decided to take off.

other hand, some ponies might realize this and become bossy with you, which is dangerous. As a novice rider, you should not be put in contact with ponies who will deliberately try to boss or hurt you, and no good riding school owner or instructor would do this.

Remember to speak when handling your pony. Use his name a lot when you approach him, or before you ask him to do something. Find out from his former owner what commands he is used to so that you do not confuse him by using different ones. Most ponies know (or should know) 'over'

Picking up a
foreleg.

Picking up a
hindleg.

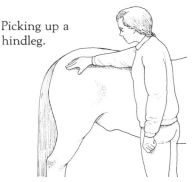

*Picking up and holding feet. Stroke the
shoulder and talk to the pony.*

Stroke the hindquarters and talk to the pony.

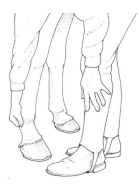

*Stroke down the leg, hold the fetlock round
the back. Lean your weight on his forearm
and at the same time say 'up' and pull the
fetlock up.*

*Stroke down the inside of the leg to the
fetlock, holding it round the back and lifting
it as for the foreleg.*

*Hold the foot with your fingers as shown so
the pony cannot put weight on you.*

*Hold the foot in your fingers like this, which
makes it uncomfortable for the pony to lean
his weight on you. When you've finished a
foot, don't just let go, put it down or the pony
may wave it around and kick you by mistake.*

(to move over in the box or elsewhere), 'walk on' (to use when leading in hand) 'whoa' (to ask him to stop and stand still). They will also know 'trot on' and 'canter'.

The trick when talking to a pony is to use simple, short commands, perhaps saying his name first, such as 'Snowy, walk on'. The pony does not understand the words, but recognizes the sounds and learns to connect certain sounds with certain actions. If you use a long string of words, for instance, 'For goodness sake, Snowy, will you behave and walk on properly', he will not be able to recognize 'walk on' so will not know what you want him to do. The only time when a quietly-spoken stream of words might be acceptable would be

when you are cuddling him and just being friendly. He will then understand that you are just being affectionate and do not want him to do anything in particular.

Ponies touch each other a lot, and appeciate it when you touch them kindly. Stroke them on the neck rather than patting them, and gently scratch their withers or stroke their ears. Lots of ponies put their heads into your arms for a cuddle or lean over your shoulder for you to scratch their withers and backs, as they would with another pony. Don't tell your pony off for this, or he will think you don't like him. Some ponies even try to scratch your back with their teeth: this is a great compliment and means that the pony completely accepts and

To catch a pony, have the bridle, headcollar or halter over your shoulder and approach from the side so he can see you clearly.

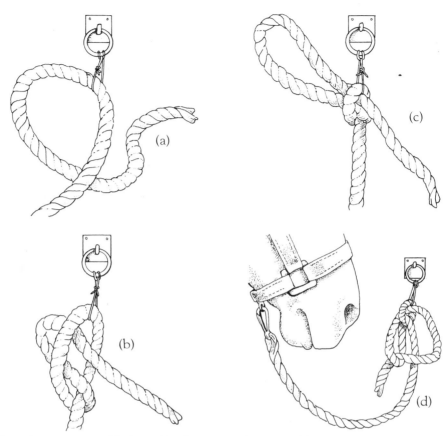

When tying up a pony, add a loop of binder twine to the ring so if the pony panics and pulls back the twine will break and the pony will get free. Use a slip knot (a–c). If you pull the loose end as shown in (c), the knot will undo at once and free the pony. Do not pass the loose end through the loop of the knot as shown in (d). If you pull the end in this position you will tighten the knot, making the slipknot impossible to free quickly in an emergency.

likes you.

If you come up against a naughty pony who bites or kicks, or really misbehaves, learn to tell him off with a stern 'no', which most ponies understand. Discuss such ponies with an expert such as your instructor, who can tell you how to recognize and deal with bad behaviour. Even with naughty ponies, one sharp smack should be enough to correct them. If you ever see anyone thrashing or beating a pony, you can be sure they are either a bully or don't understand how a pony's mind works. Ponies are not stupid but their minds work simply. To punish or praise a pony, you have to do it within no more than a second or two or he won't connect it with what he's just done. If a pony nips you, say 'no' sharply and perhaps give him a smack on the belly immediately. Don't nurse your injury first, and then start smacking him several seconds later in temper or revenge. Not only will you be showing yourself up as someone who doesn't know what they're doing, but you will also thoroughly confuse the pony, who will not understand why you are behaving like that, and you could easily make him resentful and bitter.

The same goes for praise. If he does something well say at once: 'good boy'

in a very pleased tone, and he'll understand how pleased you are and will feel happy.

Be fair with your pony. Don't tell him off for something naughty on one occasion but let him get away with it the next time or he won't know where he stands and will become uncertain. Be fair and consistent, and he'll come to trust and respect you.

Giving titbits

Titbits can lead to a lot of mis-understandings. It is best not to give a titbit when you first see your pony, otherwise you won't know whether he's greeting you for yourself or for the titbits. Do give them when he's been good, has done well, or when you are saying goodbye, but keep your fingers and thumb flat or they may be mistaken for food. Keep to set times or he

may become spiteful and always be looking for them. It is better not to give titbits from the saddle, or the pony might stop to ask for one while you are out riding and refuse to move on again when no titbit arrives, and this can be a real nuisance.

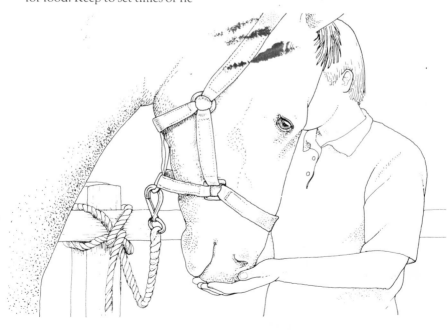

EXERCISING

Ponies are intended to be on the move. In the wild they live in all types of country from open plains to large forests, but they are never hemmed into fields or enclosures, and certainly nothing as small as a stable.

In natural conditions their space is only restricted by the extent of their grazing grounds, and once a grazing area is eaten bare the herd simply moves somewhere else. They graze naturally for about 16 hours a day, walking around as they eat. Ponies turned out in a field or paddock also do this.

Ponies need exercise and movement, and domesticated, particularly privately-owned, ponies are often kept short of exercise. Riding school ponies may get much more exercise than privately-owned ones, but it is all work, although schools which hack out can give their ponies more variety. Ponies love long hacks with other ponies. This mimics their natural herd existence, moving from one area to another with their family and friends, mostly walking or going along in a gentle canter with the occasional trot. The reason so many ponies go well in a line is that this is how they go in nature, roughly in single file. They only gallop in a bunch when being chased by a predator. In domestication, this sort of thing is seen in horses on the racecourse, which are being 'chased' or urged on by their jockeys.

Riding out to stretch your pony's legs may be regarded as exercise. Having a demanding lesson, completing a cross-country course or a course of show jumps, doing a day's hunting or attending a long, weary show, can be regarded as work to the pony – mentally and bodily tiring.

One form of exercise which should form part of every pony's daily routine, but which many are denied, is time at liberty in a paddock with at least one other pony, giving them a chance to behave naturally, to play, roll, buck and charge about doing what comes naturally.

Being confined to a stable for too long is like you being told to go to your room and not knowing when you are going to be able to come out again. It's fine being in your room for a short time doing something interesting, but you wouldn't want to spend 22 or 23 hours a day in it, would you? Or be denied playtime at school? Or the chance to talk to and play with your friends? If you think of a pony's life in this way it's easy to see just how important exercise and liberty, as opposed to just work, are to him.

It is generally felt that a stabled pony in good health should have two hours a day ridden exercise if he is not having any other form of exercise. Even two hours, which is quite a long ride, is not much relief from being stabled for the remaining 22 hours. And lots of ponies do not even have two hours' exercise.

Exercise is good for a pony's body and mind. It keeps his circulation going, transporting nutrients and oxygen round the body. Blood also carries away various waste products or natural poisons formed as a result of breathing and eating. As with people, the more a pony works the faster his heart beats, carrying blood round faster to do the extra work.

By keeping a pony well exercised,

Exercise is *very* important for your pony. Before he can work hard for you he must be made fit, and working up and down hills, as shown here, really helps to develop muscle strength and breathing, and teaches the pony to pick his feet up.

When turning a pony out into a field, lead him through the gate and then turn him back to face it, standing and stroking him for several seconds before releasing him. If he whirls round on his hind legs (as many do) and kicks up with delight, you will be well out of reach of his heels. It also stops him getting into the bad habit of charging off the second he's in the field.

you are, therefore, helping keep him in good health. Also, as his body is constantly working it gets stronger and keeps agile, and fairly fit, so he can work and carry you safely. An unfit, unhealthy pony is weak and may stumble and fall, taking you with him.

There are various ways of giving your pony exercise. Ponies on the combined system, at grass or yarded, are much more fortunate than a fully stabled pony as they can exercise when they want, and being ridden is not so important. However, hard-working ponies have to be hard and fit, and they should be ridden as well to keep their muscles used to carrying weight and working under the weight of a rider.

When you go out for a ride you should always walk for at least the first quarter of an hour, particularly if the pony has been nibbling hay or grass just before you got ready. This warms him up and prepares his muscles for harder work. Most rides should consist mainly of walking, with gentle trotting before asking for anything more strenuous such as cantering, galloping (which should be done rarely) or jumping. It is all right to trot on roads provided you do a steady trot. Ask your instructor to demonstrate what is called a 'working' trot and get this into your mind. You should never canter on roads or on hard, rough ground as this can lame your pony. It's better if you have bridleways, trails, or open spaces such as moors or beaches to ride on.

Anyone taking a pony on to public roads (which is most people) should really take the British Horse Society's

Riding and Road Safety Test or the equivalent in their country so that they know how to behave on roads and in traffic. As a novice rider, you should not ride out alone, in any case, but always have someone experienced with you.

Apart from being ridden and turned out, a pony can be exercised by lungeing, which should be done by an expert such as the livery yard owner or a qualified member of staff. Here, he walks, trots and canters around in a large circle on the end of a long lunge rein held by the trainer in the centre. Lungeing is used to train ponies to obey the voice, but well-trained, well-schooled ponies are also lunged to warm them up or to exercise them, particularly in the case of small ones whose child rider is not available and who are too small to be ridden by an adult. Half an hour of lungeing at a time is plenty, and the trainer must remember to walk the pony first to warm him up, and to change direction (called changing the rein) often so that the pony works equally to both sides.

After exercise, walk for the last quarter of an hour home. If your pony is hot and sweating when you return, you must lead him around in hand to cool him down before putting him in his stable, and especially before turning him out in his field, otherwise he might get chilled. He should be cooled down to calm him down, otherwise he might sweat up again later in his box or, more rarely, in his field, and get a chill just standing there. If it is raining, trot gently towards home to keep him warm as a warm pony will dry off quicker when you get home than a cold one.

If the pony is cool and wet and lives out, he can be turned into his field in the rain with no harm done. There is no point in drying him off, unless he is to wear a turn-out rug (see Chapter 7), as he will simply get wet again. If he does wear a rug, he must be dry under his rug, otherwise he might stay clammy and gradually get colder and colder. A stabled pony can be dried off by laying straw on his back under an old rug, or by wearing a special mesh rug called an anti-sweat rug, or in one of the modern 'breatheable' fabric rugs. Check that he is warm and dry before rugging him up properly for the night.

After exercise, see that the pony is cooled down before feeding him a short feed, although he can have a haynet to munch at, and water, while you are putting the tack away. Once he's cool give him a short feed if he has one. Ponies who are fed while hot and sweating often get indigestion (colic – see Chapter 10) which is quite serious; a bad case can even kill a pony.

Do not let anyone tell you that it's all right to keep a pony stabled without exercise. Ordinary ponies that are not working very hard do not need a day off standing doing nothing in their stables. In fact, this will do them more harm than good. Also, don't let anyone tell you that half an hour or an hour is enough exercise. It is better than nothing, but it is not enough. Do your best to keep your pony at a place where he can be turned out daily as part of his normal routine, not as a treat. If the fields are too wet ask for him to be turned loose in a manège (outdoor riding arena) or in the indoor school, if there is one, with another pony or ponies for company.

LIVERY

Livery yards will have a firmly established routine. If you keep your pony at one, he will be gradually accustomed to fit into it according to how he is to be kept.

Normally, first thing in the morning ponies are inspected to see if they have injured themselves in the night. Their water is checked (they often have the habit of doing droppings in their water or getting food and bedding in it) and they are fed and hayed up (given hay). If they are working early the hay may be left until after work. They are 'quartered' (given a light brushing over with the dandy brush, sponged and their feet picked out, to tidy them up and mucked out.

The pony may be either exercised or turned out. A stabled pony should be groomed when he has cooled down after work. Ponies may be fed again, hayed up, watered and skipped out at lunch-time, again mid-afternoon and possibly later at night, too. Rugs should be kept comfortable, if worn, on each occasion.

People looking after their own ponies may only be able to see to them morning and evening, but as long as the necessary jobs are done, this is all right. If you are riding before school, you can then give the pony a very full haynet, or even two, plus two buckets of water, to last until you get back after school to perhaps ride again, or skip out and feed, hay and water again for the night.

Ponies who are to spend the day in the field should be given their short feed, if they have one, first so they can eat it in peace. They are then turned out, being given hay in the field if it is winter. When they come in at night, they can have another very full net, plus water and perhaps a short feed if they need one. If the pony only has one short feed a day, give it at night when it will help to keep him warm and he has plenty of time to digest it.

In summer, you may reverse this routine, and bring the pony into a well-bedded loose box with plenty of hay and water during the day, turning him out again in the evening. Grooming time is up to you if he is not ridden, but it is easier to get a pony clean when his skin is slightly warm and toned up from exercise.

Grass-kept ponies must be visited and checked twice a day. In winter, hay should be given twice a day, maybe a short feed at night, and in the morning if needed. Droppings should be removed from the field shelter, if not from the land itself, and the fencing and gates checked, along with the water supply.

If you keep to the same times, more or less, each day, the pony will know what to expect and will become 'routined' in mind and body, which is better for him – and teaches you discipline.

CHAPTER 6

FOOT CARE AND SHOEING

Ponies have an advantage over us in that they have four feet instead of two. Although this means they have to learn to manage four feet and legs at the same time when they are young foals, it also means they are much better balanced and much faster than we are. They needed four healthy, tough feet in nature to escape predators, and they need those same feet to be healthy in order to work for us.

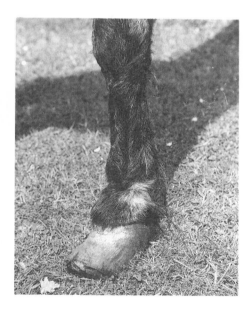

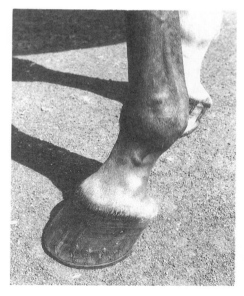

A badly neglected hoof, much too long and starting to turn up into an unnatural shape which forces the pony to go on his heels and puts strain on his legs and feet. The horn is broken and coming away. This sort of neglect can also cause laminitis, a serious foot disorder.

A well-shod hoof, neatly trimmed and with the shoe giving good support and protection to the hoof. You can see the old nail holes below the new clenches and also the ones before those near the bottom of the hoof, showing how the horn grows between shoeings.

Looking at a pony's feet, it is easy to imagine they are solid blocks of horn and that the pony can't feel discomfort or pain in his feet, but nothing could be further from the truth. Inside the outer wall of horn which you see when you look at the foot is a very sensitive, complicated system of fleshy tissue, nerves, blood and bone. The wall is lined with horny leaves rather like the underside of a mushroom, which lock into similar leaves of soft, fleshy tissue on the main foot bone. Horn (the same type of tissue as fingernails) is insensitive or 'dead', but the fleshy tissues in the feet are very much alive and can feel pressure and pain. The leaves of horn lining the wall are called the horny or insensitive laminae, and the fleshy ones the sensitive laminae. This locking together of insensitive and sensitive laminae holds the entire foot together. The sensitive laminae, in turn, are fixed to the main bone of the foot, the pedal bone.

Looking underneath the foot, you will see an up-and-down surface which helps the pony keep his grip on the ground in natural conditions. Running down the centre of the foot from the heels at the back is a rubbery, horny wedge called the frog, and surrounding it is an area called the sole. Inside the foot, there is a sensitive sole above the horny outer one and a sensitive frog above the horny frog.

The area inside the heel at the back of the foot is filled with a firm but squashy tissue called the plantar cushion. The slight bulge you see running round the top of the hoof wall is the coronet, and that is where the horn grows from.

SHOES

Because ponies work on rough or hard surfaces, such as roads, their feet wear down faster than they can grow, and they need to be fitted with metal shoes to protect them. However, if ponies work almost entirely on softish ground such as fields or surfaced riding schools, there is no need for shoes. Ponies that are resting at grass should have their shoes removed and their feet trimmed to give their feet a chance to work naturally. Ponies' feet spread or expand when weight is put on them, and it is this spreading and contracting (tightening up again) which pumps the blood round the feet and legs. Without it all sorts of foot problems can arise. Metal shoes, which are nailed on, hold the feet in, and prevent them spreading as much as they normally would when the pony puts weight on his feet. When your farrier fits your pony's shoes, he will put nails only in the front and sides of the shoes, allowing the back or heel area to expand as needed, for this reason.

YOUR FARRIER

Farriers are very skilled, strong men doing a hard, and sometimes dangerous job. They all have to be qualified and registered with the Farriers Registration Council. It takes several years' training to become a farrier, together with experience working with a fully qualified farrier.

If you keep your pony at a yard, it will have its own farrier, but some places expect owners to find their own. Your consultant will recommend a good one to you, if necessary.

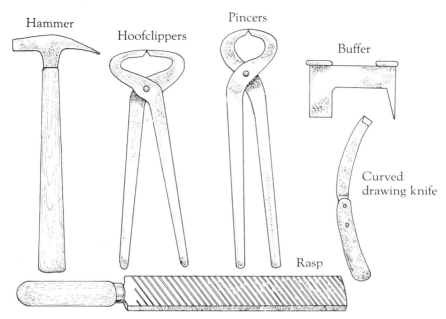

Farrier's tools.

WHAT HAPPENS DURING SHOEING

When your pony's shoes have worn down and he needs shoeing again, the farrier should first of all study each foot to see how the shoes have worn, as few ponies put their feet down and wear their shoes absolutely evenly. He will then remove the shoes. At some point the pony should be walked round so that the farrier can watch the pony move to see how he puts his feet down and wears them, so he can make corrections when fitting the shoes, if necessary and possible. With adult ponies, it is not always possible to correct faults in action.

The next step is to trim the feet, perhaps with pincers, a knife called a drawing knife, and also a giant 'nail file' called a rasp for smoothing off the feet as they cannot wear down at all when shod.

The farrier may shoe your pony 'hot' or 'cold'. Metal is easy to work into shape when red hot and many farriers travel round to stables bringing a portable forge or fire in which to heat the metal. The farrier will choose shoes which more or less fit your pony and, if needed, heat them in the fire so he can obtain an exact fit. He will then insert a rod called a pritchel into one of the nail

Hunter-type shoes good for general riding. On the right is the ground surface with one stud in a heel, the outside. On the left is the bearing surface which is flat, the part the pony stands on.

59

holes and burn the hot shoe lightly against the underneath of the pony's foot so that the metal singes or marks the horn and he can see where it touches and where it doesn't. It should touch the wall of the hoof evenly all round, and he will then hammer the shoe into shape to make sure it does.

Don't be alarmed at this burning process. The farrier should only burn on for a few seconds and as the horn is dead the pony is not hurt, although some dislike the hiss and smoke.

When the shoe fits, the farrier nails it on to the foot. The foot should never be cut to fit the shoe. He puts the nails only through the dead horn, so don't worry about this either. When the foot has been trimmed ask him to show you the 'white line'. This is the point where the insensitive laminae meet the sensitive laminae inside the foot. He shouldn't nail beyond the white line or he will go into the sensitive tissue and hurt the pony. He'll keep the nails to the outer edge of the foot, in the dead horn.

When the shoe is nailed on, he will turn down and smooth off the ends of the nails which have come out through the horn on the wall (these are then called 'clenches') and which help hold the shoe on. He will probably make a little clip of metal at the toe, for a front foot, or two towards the sides, for a hind foot, tapping them up flat against the wall, again to help keep the shoe in place.

Finally, he'll run the rasp round where the shoe and the horn meet to smooth off the horn, and the job is finished, apart from trotting the pony in hand to check that he is comfortable with his new shoes.

Farriers who shoe cold do not, obviously, burn on and may not get quite as good a fit as shoeing hot because the metal cannot be altered so easily. However, many farriers do get a very good fit, and as yours gets to know your pony he will probably make shoes for him in his forge at home and be able to provide shoes which fit very well.

LOOSE SHOES

When a shod pony walks on the road you will hear an even clip-clop, clip-clop sound, but sometimes a shoe works loose and makes a clanking noise, or tinny sound, when that foot hits the ground, so watch and see which one it is. Ponies with loose or twisted shoes must not be ridden. You should get your yard owner or parents to ask the farrier to come and see to it at once. Your instructor or yard owner should be able to remove the shoe and the pony can be ridden on soft ground or just turned out until he is reshod.

FOOT CARE

You must pick out and check your pony's feet and shoes before and after every ride. Using the hoofpick from heel to toe, gently but firmly pick out all mud, grit and stones, also droppings and bedding. Try, without pushing too hard, to get the end of the pick under the shoe at the heels. If you can, and if the shoe can be moved about, it is loose and must be tightened up or removed and replaced.

If a pony's shoes are not too badly

Shoes and studs

Most ponies and horses are shod with shoes which are based upon a design called the hunter shoe. It is ridged and shaped to give a good grip and lessen the chance of its being sucked off in mud. At the heels of the shoe there may be holes into which you can screw different sorts of studs. These are little metal squares or points which are used for different ground conditions such as slippery roads, deep mud, hard earth and so on, to help the pony work securely without falling down. Studs should not be left in (except for tiny road studs) as they tilt the pony's feet slightly, which is uncomfortable unless the ground conditions need them. Remove studs as soon as work on that ground is finished, and plug the holes with oily cotton wool to stop them becoming clogged with soil and grit.

Shoes can be made with a hole in one or both heels, like this, for different types of stud to be screwed in. Where only one hole is made it goes on the outside branch of the shoe, as here. You can tell the outside from the inside branch because the outside normally has four nails in it, the inside usually has only three.

worn when the time comes round for his feet to be trimmed (which will be every six weeks) the farrier can take them off, trim back the horn, and replace the same shoes. This is cheaper than having new shoes.

Watch for clenches rising up out of their holes, horn growing over the shoe, shoes getting thin or working forward from the heels, or the horn cracking round the bottom. All these are signs that the pony needs shoeing again.

Take care of your pony's feet between farrier visits, so you can spot any problems. Look also for soft, soggy horn or a bad smell, either of which can mean that your pony has a foot disease. When riding, he may

seem lame or reluctant to work. He can get such a disease, called thrush, from standing too long on dirty, wet bedding or from being out all the time on a very wet, muddy field.

Don't take your pony fast over rough ground as he can bruise his feet through the horny sole. Also don't ride him if he is much in need of shoeing as this, too, can hurt him.

Your farrier is very valuable in keeping your pony comfortable and able to be ridden. Take care of your pony's feet yourself and show an interest in his work – and get your parents to pay his bills quickly – and he should be willing to help you out in an emergency, such as a lost or loose shoe.

CHAPTER 7

TACK, CLOTHING AND OTHER EQUIPMENT

A neatly kept and well organized tack room, showing saddles on brackets, bridles on round brackets, which keep the headpieces in good shape and don't crease and crack them (as might happen on a narrow peg), a ceiling hook for cleaning bridles and stirrup leathers, and a rug chest at the back. There are two saddle horses (stands) for storing or cleaning saddles, with shelves underneath for equipment.

The range of saddles and bridles, rugs
and general stable equipment is vast,
and it is impossible here to show you
more than your main requirements.
Much of the equipment available is
not really necessary, but you will
surely want and need the following
items.

SADDLES

There are various sorts of saddles, but
the best to start out with, and which
will do very well for all sorts of riding
whether on the flat or over jumps, is a
general purpose saddle, so called
because it can be used for general
riding.

Saddles are very expensive, but a
good one is essential if you are to be
positioned correctly on the pony and
the pony himself is to be comfortable.
Buy your tack from a saddler who is a
member of a professional saddle-
makers organization so you can be
sure of good quality equipment and
expert advice, and also of a good
repair service when needed. In the UK
the Society of Master Saddlers has an
oval badge which members will show
on their catalogues and in their shops.

Saddles are mainly made of leather
padding on a wooden and metal frame
called the tree. The different parts of
the saddle are shown in the pictures in
this chapter.

To keep the saddle on you'll need a
girth, a long strap with buckles at each
end. Girths can be made of leather,
natural fabrics like lampwick, or
synthetic material. Lampwick or
mohair girths are good as they absorb
the pony's sweat, and are comfortable
for him. Some girths are made of
cotton or nylon string, and some,

**The stirrup leather in place on the
stirrup bar, with the buckle right up to
the bar, as it should be, and the spare
end of the leather tucked into its
leather loop (called the keeper) on the
saddle flap behind the rider's leg.**

which are not very good and can rub
and break, are made of jute webbing.

You will also need stirrups and
stirrup leathers to support your feet
and legs. The leathers loop over the
stirrup bar under the saddle skirt: the
bar has a little catch on the end which
it is best to leave down so that should
you fall the stirrup leather will slide off
the bar, freeing you if you fall
awkwardly.

Your stirrups should be 2·5 cm (1 in)
wider than the sole of your riding boot
or shoe at its widest part, so that there
is very little chance of your foot either
becoming stuck in the stirrup in a fall,
or sliding through and trapping you
by the ankle. Stainless steel stirrups

Parts of a saddle.

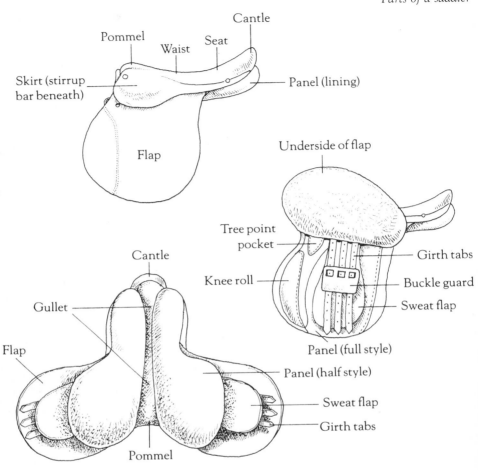

Pommel

Waist Seat Cantle

Skirt (stirrup bar beneath)

Panel (lining)

Flap

Underside of flap

Tree point pocket

Knee roll

Girth tabs

Buckle guard

Sweat flap

Panel (full style)

Cantle

Gullet

Flap

Panel (half style)

Sweat flap

Girth tabs

Pommel

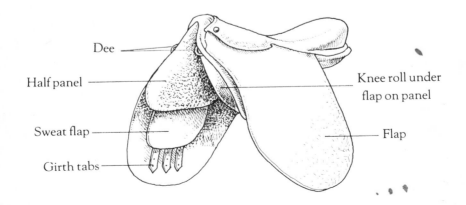

Dee

Half panel

Knee roll under flap on panel

Sweat flap

Flap

Girth tabs

Above and right: pony Club camp is a great way to spend lots of time with your pony and not have to fit him in round school, homework or other calls on your time. You have expert help and instruction on hand all the time, you can build up a really close bond with your pony and have a great time as well.

Previous page: most ponies want and need company. Solitary ones spend time moping by the fence or gate, often looking yearningly out at civilization – the stable yard, a distant field with animals in it, or even humans – to appease their loneliness. Some may resort to jumping out, with the risk of injury to themselves and others, plus damage to property.

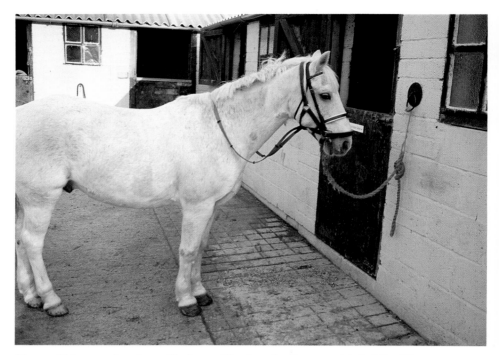

Above: this pony has been tied up with a headcollar over his bridle. The reins have been passed up through the throatlatch to keep them safely out of the way. The headcollar, though, is too big, with the noseband coming much too near the nostrils. The pony could easily remove it either accidentally or on purpose.

Left: a nicely-fitted leather headcollar, with the noseband the right height and loose enough for the pony to move his jaws comfortably when feeding, but not so loose that he could get the headcollar off.

Right: a poorly-fitted snaffle bridle. The bit is a little too high in the mouth and is wrinkling the corners of the mouth too much. The cavesson noseband is also too high and is rubbing the underneath of the face bones: it should come half way between these bones and the corners of the mouth. The browband is too high and is cutting into the base of the ears: it is also too short and is pulling the headpiece into the ears at the back. The cheekpiece buckle will prevent the browband being fitted lower, but if the cheekpieces on both side were let down a hole the browband could be lowered and the bit would be more comfortable. The throatlatch is correctly fitted, loosely enough to allow the width of four fingers between it and the jawbone.

Below: this horse is wearing a snaffle bridle with an eggbutt bit and cavesson noseband. He is also wearing a roller and has side-reins fitted from the bit to the roller. Some trainers do fit the side-reins crossed, like this, the left rein fastened to the right side of the roller and vice versa, but others feel it makes a horse too stiff and fixed in the head, neck and mouth. This method is, though, a good one to use when leading in hand a horse or pony who bites his leader, as the reins make this more difficult for him.

Above: the stirrup bar over which the stirrup leathers go to support the stirrups. The little catch on the right-hand end is normally left down so that should you fall and your foot is caught in the stirrup, the leather will be pulled off the bar and you will not be dragged.

Above: a security freeze-mark on a pony's back. Freeze-marking, and registering the number with the freeze-marking company, is an excellent way of preventing your pony being stolen, and of recovering him if he is. The companies usually offer a reward which is so generous as to ensure the return of the pony.

Right: Dante looks bright and alert and is taking a healthy interest in the photographer.

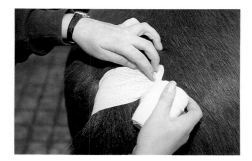

Left: start off a tail bandage by leaving up part of the bandage, like this.

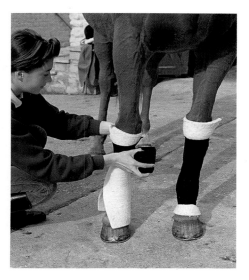

Left: putting on stable bandages. Put plenty of padding on the leg (it will slip less if you slightly damp the leg hair) and learn the knack of keeping it in place while also starting off the bandage!

Below left: continue bandaging down the leg, covering half the previous 'turn' of bandage with each new turn to help ensure it stays put.

Below: at the fetlock, bring the bandage well under the fetlock at the back, and you'll find the bandage takes a natural turn upwards again as you carry on.

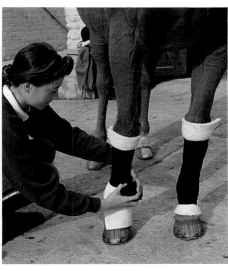

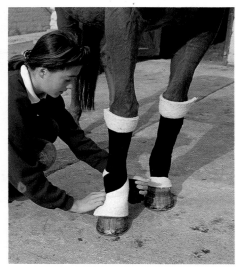

Above: loose boxes arranged down an aisle in a large building. This system provides more protection for horses, ponies and attendants in extreme weather, (very hot summers or cold winters) or prolonged periods of rain, but breathing problems can be more common in animals kept like this, unless the ventilation in the building is very good. Fresh air is vital to the health of ponies.

Above: a corner of a stable yard. Loose boxes are often built in rows at right angles to each other, sometimes forming a complete square with an attractive archway or gate entrance. This system means the yard is sheltered from wind and rain.

Below: a loose box must be roomy enough to allow the horse to turn round, lie down, roll, sleep flat out and get up in safety and comfort.

Above: it is best never to ride in dusk or dark conditions, but if you have no choice, do equip yourself and your horse with reflective gear such as this exercise sheet. Your most important item of equipment, however, is a strong stirrup light showing white to the front and red to the rear, fixed to your right stirrup.

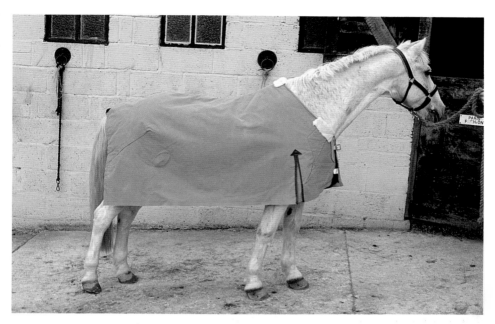

Above: a modern, shaped turn-out rug kept in place by means of its fit and leg straps without the need for an uncomfortable surcingle.

Below: a shaped, well-fitting stable rug with a comfortable, modern fastening of cross-over belly surcingles. It is quilted for winter warmth and the pony looks very cosy.

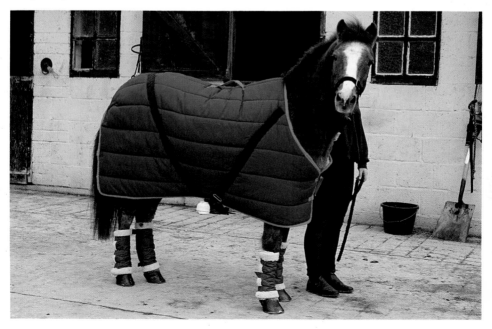

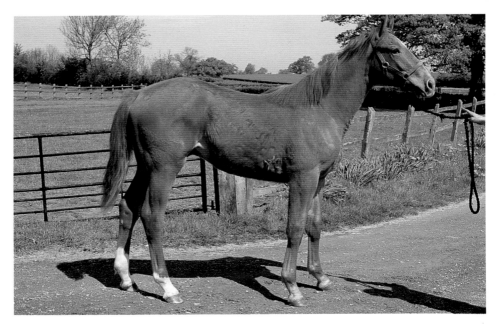

Above: this coat is dull and rough and the animal is in poor condition, skinny without her ribs actually showing.

Below: this pony has been given a blanket clip, leaving a patch of hair on his back, loins and quarters corresponding to where a blanket would go: his leg hair has also been left on.

Left: this pony is wearing a vulcanite pelham bit with roundings. The throatlatch is too tight on this bridle.

Below: put the saddle on top of the withers and slide it back into place, smoothing the hair back as you do so, so it is comfortable for the pony. The numnah is rather too large, but better that than too small.

Above: for gymkhana games many riders like a pony to be a little too small for them, like this one, as he will be easier to vault on and off. The pony is wearing a flash noseband and standing martingale. The flash helps prevent him opening his mouth too far and evading the bit and the standing martingale prevents him carrying his head too high for control. Both these pieces of tack indicate that the riding or schooling are not as good as they could be, and although mounted games offer great excitement, many experts feel that they do not encourage good horsemanship.

Opposite: jumping is one of the more exciting things you can do with your pony, but remember he has to be fit before he can jump like this safely and with enjoyment for both of you – so don't skimp on your fitness programme.

Above: a pony of classic Exmoor colouring with its beige (known as 'mealy') markings round the muzzle and eyes and on the underside of its body. None of Britain's native ponies are actually wild. They all live naturally but are all owned by someone.

are the best, being the strongest, and therefore the safest. Other metals can easily bend and break.

BRIDLES

The sole purpose of the bridle is to help you control the pony, usually by holding the bit up in his mouth, although there are bridles without bits. The parts of a bridle and how to use it are illustrated. Bridles come in various sizes, from Small Pony to Full (horse) size and can be adjusted by means of the various buckles. If you tell your saddler the height of your pony, he should supply the right size and will change it should it not fit.

A good-quality bridle really sets off a pony's appearance, and ponies, as opposed to horses, can get away with varied colours and patterns of browband. For everyday, coloured plastic is the most practical if you

To check the fit of a saddle, have the pony's heaviest rider mounted and leaning forward. There should be a gap of at least three fingers' width between the pommel and his withers.

The saddle should go in the position of the continuous line. The dotted and dashed lines show the saddle positioned too far forward and too far back.

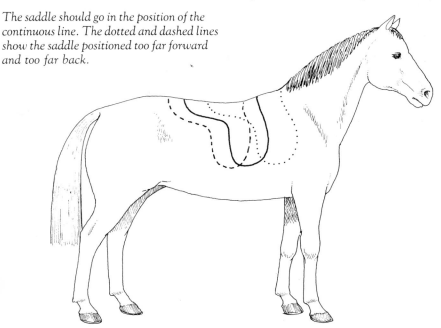

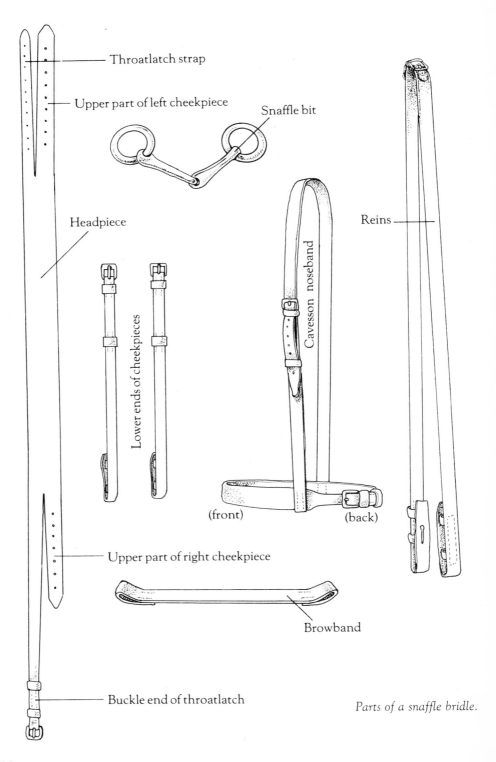

Throatlatch strap

Upper part of left cheekpiece

Snaffle bit

Headpiece

Reins

Lower ends of cheekpieces

Cavesson noseband

(front)

(back)

Upper part of right cheekpiece

Browband

Buckle end of throatlatch

Parts of a snaffle bridle.

don't want leather, but for shows velvet or satin can be used.

A good first pony will not need a noseband on his bridle, but may look unfinished without one. He should only need a plain noseband, called a 'cavesson'. More difficult ponies can have different nosebands which aim to give more control, and your instructor will explain about these as you gain more knowledge.

It is important that the reins feel comfortable in your hands, neither too wide nor too narrow, so try a few widths in the shop or at the yard. Most people like reins with a roughened laced pattern, or rubber covered, to give a firm hold, especially

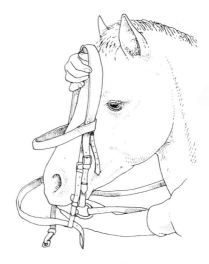

Two ways to put on a bridle. Top: Hold the headpiece in your right hand (usually with your arm under the pony's throat unless he's very small) and rest the bit in your left hand, pressing it lightly against his teeth where they meet, when he should open his mouth. You then raise the headpiece, bringing the bit up into his mouth, and carefully bring the headpiece over the ears one at a time, using your left hand as well. Bottom: For a difficult pony, hold the cheekpieces together with your right hand on his face to control his head. Use your left thumb in the corner of his mouth, wiggling it about, to get him to open his mouth. When he does, slip in the bit and proceed as normal.

A properly fitting snaffle bridle with cavesson noseband. The browband is long enough to allow plenty of room for the ears and does not pull the headpiece into the back of them, the throatlatch is loose enough to allow the pony to flex at the poll (you should be able to get four fingers' width between it and his face), the noseband is mid-way between his sharp face bones and the corners of his mouth, and the bit is touching the corners of the mouth and not hanging too low.

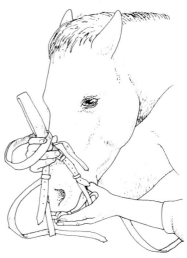

A well-fitting pelham bridle – plenty of room round the ears and the noseband not too high. The bit is a comfortable height in the mouth. Pelham bits are stronger in action than snaffles, because they have a chain (called a curb chain) seen here just above the pony's chin, in the groove called the chin groove. It is attached to hooks on the top part of the bit and when the curb reins (the bottom reins) are used, the chain tightens in the chin groove, holding the pony's bottom jaw between the chain and the bit mouthpiece. Ponies have to be taught by an expert to obey this different feel, but once they understand, you will have more control over a strong pony than with a snaffle.

in wet weather when plain leather can slip through your hands even if you wear gloves.

NECKSTRAP

It is sensible to use a neckstrap on your pony to give you something to hold on to if you feel in need of it. This is much better than hanging on to the reins and hurting the pony's mouth. The neckstrap fits round the bottom of the pony's neck, like a collar, and fastens to the saddle, as shown in the picture.

THE BIT

The metal, plastic or rubber bit in your pony's mouth is very important, as his mouth is sensitive and easily hurt. The bits shown should both be

A neckstrap fastened to the little metal loops (called dees) on the pommel is an excellent idea. You can hold on to it if you need to keep yourself steady, without hanging on the reins and hurting the pony's mouth.

suitable for a first pony, and your pony's former owner should tell you what sort of bit the pony prefers. Your instructor will also be able to help with this.

Bits of a type called snaffle have just one mouthpiece (the part of the bit going through the pony's mouth is called the mouthpiece). The mouthpiece may be jointed in the middle, and some ponies like this fairly loose feel. Or, it may be slightly curved which leaves room for the tongue and some ponies prefer the steadier feel that this bit gives.

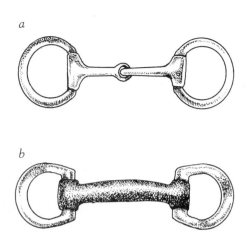

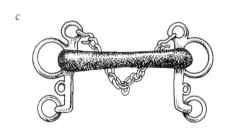

Types of bit: (a) eggbutt jointed snaffle, (b) eggbutt half-moon (or mullen mouthed) snaffle, (c) straight bar pelham with curb chain, (d) loose ring jointed snaffle, (e) loose ring half-moon (or mullen mouthed) snaffle.

All bits rest on the pony's lower jaw over his tongue, just where the corners of his mouth are, on a part of his gum which has no teeth. Ask your instructor to show you the inside of a pony's mouth but don't try to look on your own as he might accidentally nip your fingers. A large part of learning to ride involves learning to use the bit gently with steady hands, so as to 'talk' to the pony through signals given down the reins and felt by the pony through the bit in his mouth. Never jab the pony in the mouth or try to pull hard on the reins as this can hurt him and is very bad riding.

HEADCOLLAR

A headcollar with a clip-on leadrope is like a heavyweight bridle with no bit and probably no browband. You use it for leading the pony about and for trying him up if this is needed. They are made in leather or nylon webbing (cheaper) and can be adjusted by the buckle at the side.

RUGS

There are two main types of rugs and you may not need either of them. There are stable rugs for indoor use and turn-out rugs (often called New Zealand rugs because of a design which originated there) to put on the pony when he is turned out in winter.

Rugs are meant for keeping your pony warm. If he is a tough, native-type pony and not clipped much in winter, he will probably not need a rug. However, you may well need a couple of rugs if your pony has Arab or Thoroughbred blood; if he has

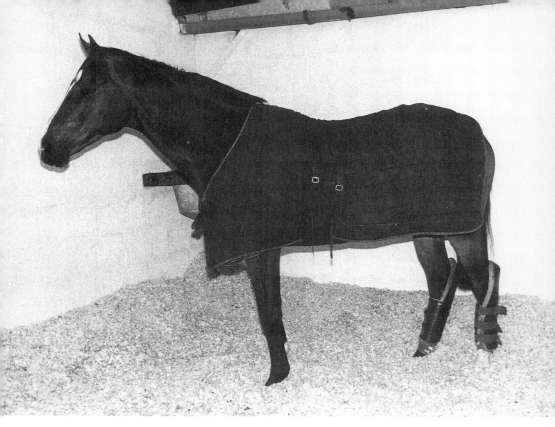

A quilted nylon stable rug kept on by a sewn-on, wide surcingle on elasticated straps. This is much more comfortable than a separate surcingle or roller but not so comfortable as the cross-over belly surcingles.

quite an extensive clip, or if he is turned out a lot in winter.

All good rugs, whether stable or turn-out rugs, should be shaped to fit the pony. The seam which goes along his backbone should rise and dip to allow room for his withers at the front, dipping down for his back, rising again for his croup and dipping towards the root of his tail again. In addition, shaping darts at elbow and stifle help take up slack and provide really good shaping and fit. These rugs are kept in place by various designs of straps (surcingles) which criss-cross under his belly and/or between his hind legs, and can be adjusted with clips or buckles, as illustrated.

Old-fashioned rugs are often not properly shaped, and are kept on by means of a surcingle which goes round the pony's girth area or middle. These are obviously much less comfortable, and they do not keep the rug on properly. Separate, padded surcingles called rollers are slightly better, but neither is as good as a well-shaped, modern rug with criss-cross surcingles. With these there is no rubbing or pressing on the backbone as they don't go over that area, and they can be fastened fairly loosely, unlike a belt-type surcingle, as the rug's shaping helps keep it in place.

Rugs: (a) a badly designed turn-out rug (often called a New Zealand). It is too tight round the neck and pulls on the withers, it is unshaped so it needs an uncomfortable surcingle (belt) round the middle to help keep it on and is not recommended. (b) the old-fashioned way of fastening on a rug with a separate blanket underneath, and a roller (like a belt) holding both rug and blanket in place. (c) a well-shaped, modern turn-out rug of quilted man-made fabric with an under-belly harness to keep it on. (d) a modern quilted stable rug with surcingles which fasten fairly loosely, criss-crossing under the belly, to keep the rug in place. This one also has hindleg straps and a belly harness (again fastened fairly loosely) for extra security.

Most rugs nowadays are made of man-made fabrics which are easy to wash and dry, and they are the best type to get. You will need two, so that you can use one while washing the other. You should wash stable rugs whenever they start looking dirty; put them in a washing-machine on a warm temperature setting, and use a non-biological, mild washing product. Turn-out rugs can also often be washed in a machine, but will probably need to be re-waterproofed afterwards with a product from your saddler (normally a spray or brush-on sort). Most people only wash these (often simply by hosing them down on the outside during the winter to remove mud) every month or so and vacuum the lining, as it's impossible to keep them really clean. Again, you should really have two unless you have somewhere warm to spread a turn-out rug overnight to dry for the next day.

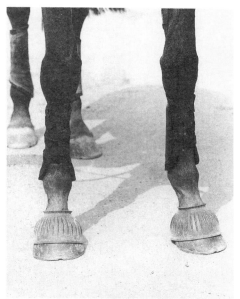

This horse is wearing tendon boots to protect his tendons from knocks from his own back feet. They do not actually support tendons during work. On his feet he is wearing rubber over-reach boots to protect his heels from being trodden on and injured by his back feet. Boots like these are often worn during fast work and jumping, when such injuries might happen.

BOOTS AND BANDAGES

Protective boots and bandages are designed to protect your pony from knocks he gives himself. When working fast, twisting and turning, or jumping, any pony can kick himself and cut his leg, and you should discuss with your instructor whether or not he or she thinks your pony could need boots or bandages.

Ponies which hit themselves on the inside of their legs are said to 'brush' and you can buy brushing boots (see picture) which protect against this. Speedicutting is the word used when they hit themselves higher up under the knee or hock and speedicutting

boots, slightly longer than brushing boots, are also available. Both these boots fit with a hard shield or firm padding over the fetlock joint and up the inside of the leg, and fasten with straps having either buckles or clips.

Over-reach boots (bell-shaped rubber or plastic) are for ponies who tread on their front heels with their hind feet. If your pony needs them, buy the sort which strap on round the pastern rather than the type which have to be pulled on over the hoof as those are very difficult to cope with.

Bandages for work, called exercise bandages, need a lot of skill to put on

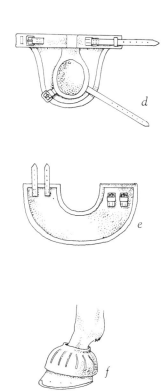

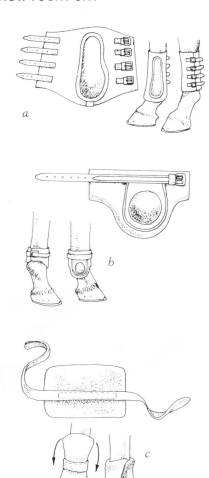

Boots: (a) brushing boots, (b) fetlock boots, (c) Yorkshire boots, (d) knee pads, (e) an over-reach boot of the type which straps on – much easier to use than the pull-on sort, (f) ordinary over-reach boot.

and you would do best to use boots instead until you have more experience. They are normally made of stretchy material called crepe and are put on over padding for protection.

Stable bandages are longer, wider and made of woollen material. Also put on over padding, they are used for extra warmth or to dry off wet legs. It is useful to know how to use these and the diagrams show you how.

Bandaging is one skill best learnt in a lesson from your instructor together with practice, as it is important to put them on with even pressure.

Tail bandages are not essential, either. They are used at grooming on a slightly damped dock to keep the hair smooth and close on a pulled tail. If you do not put them on evenly, they will give the hair a crinkly effect worse than not using a tail bandage at all. Put on too tightly they can seriously injure the tail. They are also used when travelling to protect against rubs should the pony steady himself by leaning on his quarters.

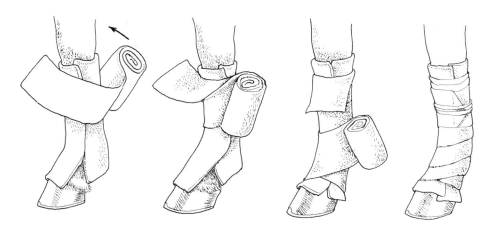

Putting on stable bandages. Damp the leg hair slightly to help the padding stay in place during bandaging. Wrap your padding snugly round the leg and lay the end of the bandage across the leg, winding the roll round the back and over itself again at the side. The loose end is now turned down and you can bandage over it. Try to finish your bandage with the pointed end pointing backwards. Fasten the tapes in a firm bow no tighter than the bandage itself, and tuck in the spare ends.

Putting on a tail bandage. Put the end of the bandage under the tail. (You can dampen the tail hairs slightly to help keep it in place, but not the bandage as it may shrink and become uncomfortably tight.) Make sure the bandage is right up under the root of the tail. Bandage over the spare end and a little above it, then keep bandaging down about two-thirds of the way down the dock. Don't stretch the bandage much as you work. Finish off by tying the tapes no tighter than the bandage itself. Tie the bow at the side of the tail so the pony doesn't bruise his dock should he lean on the bow. Tuck in the ends and cover them with a turn of bandage, for neatness and safety.

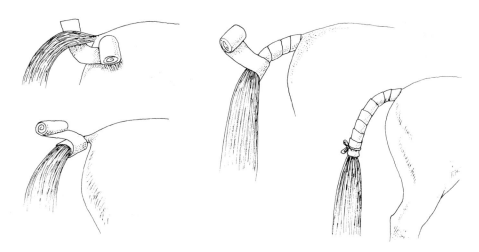

CLEANING LEATHER TACK

All leather tack, from saddles to straps on boots, is cleaned the same way. You'll need the following: bucket, leather dressing, chamois leather, folded rubber, glycerine saddle soap two sponges (one for washing, one for soaping), so collect them together before you start.

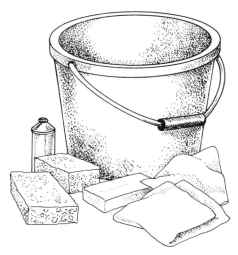

Dip the washing sponge into a bucket of just-warm water and firmly rub all dirt and grease off the saddle. If it is muddy remove the mud gently as it will otherwise scratch the leather permanently. With a blunt knife or coin, carefully scrape off hardened, black little lumps of grease (called 'jockeys') on the underside of the leather which touches the pony.

Now take the soap sponge, wet the saddle soap not the sponge, and rub some soap on the sponge. Using firm circular movements, or back-and-forth movements for straps, work the saddle soap into the leather, building up a sheen as the soap sinks in. If the soap lathers it is too wet. The soap is meant to condition and protect the leather, not wash it. Do this all over the leather, particularly on the most absorbent underside, and pay special attention to folded parts such as where the bridle cheekpieces curve round the bit rings.

As you work, watch out for worn or rotting stitching, which must be repaired by a saddler before using it again, otherwise it could give way and cause an accident.

Before taking the bridle to pieces, make sure that you know how to put it together again by practising beforehand with the aid of the diagrams. Otherwise, you can simply move the buckles down a hole instead of taking it all to pieces to get at the leather where the buckles press on, putting it back afterwards. Use a matchstick to poke soap out of holes on straps.

Clean the girth in the same way if it is leather. If it is fabric, scrub it with warm water, soap and a nailbrush, rinse it very thoroughly and hang it up by both sets of buckles to dry so the water doesn't run down on to one set and rust them.

Wash your stirrups, and every so often clean them with metal polish. You can clean your bit rings with polish but never get polish on or near the mouthpiece, or on to leather if cleaning buckles.

When you have finished, put everything back together again and hang the bridle on a proper bracket so that it retains its shape (an empty saddle soap tin will do nicely), and hang your saddle on a saddle rack, as shown, perhaps covered with a stable rubber or piece of old sheet. Tack should be stored in a warmish, dry place or it will go mouldy and rot.

OTHER EQUIPMENT

You will need your own grooming kit for your pony, as each should have his own to help prevent the spread of disease. Mucking-out tools will be provided by the yard, if you use one.

You can feed your pony from a bucket, if you wish, but make sure it is a wide one (obtainable from saddlers, tack stores or agricultural shops) and not the narrow household sort. If you prefer a manger (perhaps because your pony throws his bucket around), get the sort that fits across a corner which the pony cannot knock himself on. You can give water from a bucket, or automatic waterers may be installed in the loose boxes at your yard. You may need to buy your own buckets and mangers, or the stable might provide them.

Hay can be fed loose on the floor, but this is wasteful if the pony tramples it around; or it can be fed from a haynet or a hayrack. Corner-type racks are safer than others as the pony is much less likely to bang his head on them. You won't have to buy your own rack if keeping your pony in someone else's yard, but you may

have to supply a net if you are going to use one.

A useful little item is a salt-lick holder. Ponies need salt and it's a good plan to have a block of salt (called a salt lick) on the wall at the pony's muzzle height for him to lick as he wishes. Don't place it over his water as, if he bites off a chunk and it falls in the water, he will then not drink it. The holder must be of plastic or plastic-covered as the metal ones go green and taint the salt.

This is all the basic tack and equipment you will need. As you go on, you'll find that there is a very great deal of equipment you could buy for your pony which you may find useful, but which is not essential. It can be very expensive kitting out one pony and there is no point in getting carried away on items you don't really need. Especially with tack, nosebands and other items, you'll often see your favourite riders using a particular piece of equipment and want one for your own pony. However, you should discuss anything different with your instructor first as you can, in fact, do a lot of harm using the wrong equipment on a pony who doesn't need it.

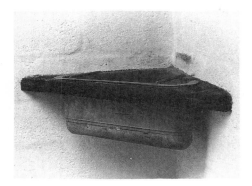

A metal corner manger with side bars across the corners to stop the pony scooping food out. It is fixed into a strong holder and the bottom edge of the manger is rounded off so the pony does not injure his knees on it.

CHAPTER 8

THE STABLE

A stable protects the pony from the weather all the year round and provides him with shelter from flies in summer; keeps him cleaner than he would be if at grass all the time; isolates him or makes nursing him easier if he is ill; and keeps him from bullying fieldmates at such a time. It also keeps him handy for us when we want to work him. A stable is also useful for bringing in a pony who must have his time on grass cut down when the grass is too rich for him, such as in spring (see Chapter 9).

A stable should have plenty of space, and be well ventilated and well drained. A pony can become ill in poor stabling.

Most horses and ponies are kept in 'loose boxes' ('box stalls' in the USA), in which there is enough room for them to move around. These are single compartments, or individual huts, which the pony may have to himself or, if the box is big enough, can share with another pony. For example, two small ponies can easily share a large, horse-sized loose box

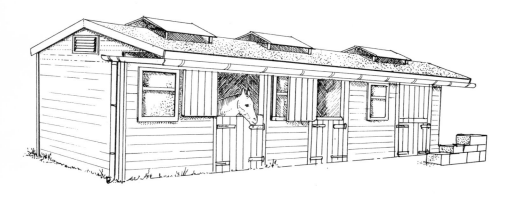

A row of modern loose boxes (called box stalls in the USA). There are ridge-roof ventilators to allow rising, stale air to escape, louvre ventilators high up on the gable ends for the same purpose and guttering and a downspout so that rainwater is guided away and doesn't run down the front of the roof on to the ground. The top doors are open as they should nearly always be when the ponies are in. Windows should also be open. The mounting block is very useful for mounting without causing the pony discomfort and pulling the saddle round. It's no disgrace to use a mounting block: it shows you are considerate of your pony's comfort.

Position the pony straight at the doorway to the loose box and lead him in that way. If you lead him in crooked he may bang his hips on the sides of the door which will hurt him and could make him difficult to bring in.

and be quite happy provided they are friends.

An old-fashioned way of keeping horses or ponies, still in use in some yards where the animals are given a lot of exercise, such as in police or army stables or town-based firms who do deliveries by horse and vehicle, is to tie them up in individual stalls, called standing stalls, tie-stalls or just stalls. In these, the pony cannot turn round but can turn his head to see behind him; he can lie down and get up and should have enough room to lie flat out to sleep properly (ponies can only sleep lightly standing up). Stalls are obviously much more restricting for the pony and are not recommended for privately-owned ponies, which are

unlikely to have more than two hours exercise a day. Some riding centres use them for ponies that are only in at night and this may just be acceptable. If you cannot be given a loose box for your pony, you should look for somewhere else to keep him.

As you can see from the picture, a loose box has a door in two halves (called 'leaves'); the top leaf is nearly always kept open for ventilation so that the stale air has a way out and fresh air can get in. Fresh air is absolutely essential to your pony's health. His lungs must be healthy if he is to breathe properly during work and rest, and they will not be if he has to live in a stuffy loose box with muggy, germ-filled air and fumes given off by his urine and droppings. As well as the top door being open, there should be a window. The design of window is normally that shown. It is called a Sheringham window, and it opens up and in to direct cool air in without causing a draught straight on to the pony. However, many top yards have differently designed windows. As long as the box is big enough for the pony to move away from any draught, he will come to no harm, particularly if he is a hardy type of pony.

The bottom door should be a comfortable height so that the pony can see out without craning his neck, but not so low he can easily jump out, and there should be no gap under the door which can cause a draught on the floor.

The best position for the window is on the opposite side of the box from the door (although few are) as this creates a draught, which will bring more air in and out, but many stables do not have this sort of layout. You can easily create a cross-draught if the owner of the yard will let you, just by removing one plank or brick high up on the back wall. Try to have a box which also has louvres (slats of wood which can be opened and closed) somewhere in the box on an outside wall and keep them open. Another feature which encourages good ventilation is called a 'ridge roof ventilator'. This is an extra small roof on the top of the ridge (the highest point of a two-sided roof) over an opening which lets out the warm, stale air. Warm air always rises, so this is a particularly good ventilation point.

Most stable floors are of concrete, which is rather hard and cold but all

right if it is kept clean, the bed is properly managed, and there is a slight slope to the floor so that urine has a chance to drain out of the box to a nearby drain. To test this, when the box is free of bedding, tip a bucket of water in the very middle of the floor and see where it drains to. If it forms a pool in the centre of the box, or runs into a corner where there is no outlet, the drainage is not good enough. If there were urine soaking the bedding, the box would soon become smelly and most unhealthy. Much urine is soaked up by the bedding, but even so good drainage helps keep a healthy air space in the box.

Stables should be in an area where water will not drain into them from surrounding land, and the floor level should always be a little higher than the yard outside. Most local planning authorities insist on certain drains in the yard but this will be taken care of by the yard owner.

How big should a box be? For a small pony under 12 hands high, a stable of about 2 m (6 ft 6 in) square is suitable, going up to 3 m (about 10 ft) square for a 14·2 hands high pony. Don't be fobbed off with a too-small box – anything less than these sizes will mean the pony cannot move around, lie down and get up, and maybe roll, comfortably or even safely. He might get cast and become scared of lying down to rest. As for height, most stables are too low and this can be dangerous as it results in bad ventilation, and may make the pony feel uncomfortably closed in. There should be at least 1 m (yd) above the top of the pony's ears when he is standing with his head up naturally, and preferably more.

Stables can be of wood, brick, stone, strong concrete blocks or reinforced concrete and some are of strong artificial materials. Metal and asbestos are very unsuitable as they retain the cold and damp in winter and the heat in summer. The roof should be of wood, ideally double thickness (difficult to check!) with roofing tiles, slates or special insulated roofing felt. Your parents will best be able to check up on how the stable is made – but whatever it is made of, it must be strong as ponies can easily kick a hole in, or even bring down, a weak building.

Getting cast

When a pony gets down and folds his legs against the stable wall he cannot stretch them out to get up again. This is called 'being cast'. Cast ponies may struggle and injure themselves trying to get up. If your pony becomes cast, fetch expert help at once. Banking the bedding up in a thick 'cushion' round the wall helps prevent his getting cast.

CHAPTER 9

FIELD MANAGEMENT

If you keep your pony on someone else's land you may not have much control over how they look after the grass, but if you know the basic points of good land management you will at least know whether they are taking reasonable care of the paddocks your pony has to graze on.

Ponies are known as 'selective grazers', in other words they are fussy about what they will eat. This is because nature has given them delicate digestive systems and bad food can make them ill. They pick out lavatory areas in a field, and will not eat the grass in these areas. The grass here, therefore, grows long, tough and loses its sweetness.

The areas where they feed, therefore, can become over-grazed – eaten down to the soil so that the grass has no chance to grow again unless the field is rested. If a field is no longer producing much grass, but merely

It is important for horses and ponies to be able to go out and exercise in a field and enjoy themselves, but their hooves do cut up the ground, especially in wet weather. This is one reason why paddocks must be rested and treated, so they have a chance to grow and recover.

acting as an exercise area this is very wasteful as well-cared for grass is much cheaper than bought-in food such as hay and concentrates, and ponies in light to medium work can live very well off grass for much of the year.

It's generally accepted that one pony needs 1 hectare (about 2 acres) of land if he is to be out on it all year, with half that much for each additional pony or horse. This is a rough measurement but a fair guide. Most riding centres and private owners do not have enough land, worked out on this basis, and have to provide extra food, especially in winter. But however small your area of land is, try to divide it into two or more sections, if possible, so you can graze and rest each part in turn, giving the grass a chance to grow. The driest areas could be kept as a winter field as they will be less likely to become very muddy in wet weather.

The ponies should spend a few weeks using one paddock (maybe taking it in turns to be turned out in groups if they don't all get on with each other) while the other is resting (i.e., no ponies on it at all during this time). When a field has been grazed for a few weeks, and the grass starts to look very patchy, close this field up and put the ponies on to the other one.

The landowner should now cut the grass left over and harrow the field. A harrow roots out the dead matted grass. The land could then receive a dressing of fertilizer and must be rested for a few weeks to let the grass recover and grow again. Then the ponies go back on it to rest the second field, and so on.

This rotation system is the basis of land management. If you have your own land or have rented some for several months or years, it is worth getting advice, and a proper care timetable, from the government agricultural department (the Equine Services Department of the Agricultural Development Advisory Service (ADAS) which is part of your local Ministry of Agriculture in the UK), or from a firm selling fertilizers. The goverment agriculture department's local office telephone number will be in the telephone directory, and you can find fertilizer firms' numbers from farmers' suppliers, from the government advisory service, or by reading the local farming papers.

Some people think that the quality of grass for ponies does not matter and it's not worth giving it any care. This is not true. It is much cheaper to look after your grass, and much nicer for the ponies, than to put them on a plot of land which is nothing but a dust bowl in summer or a mud bath in winter because it has not been cared for. If the ponies become hungry, too, they could start jumping out or getting into trouble.

It is true that ponies don't need, indeed cannot take, rich grass like that used for milking cows. This can cause them to get colic or laminitis (a serious foot disease). Ponies are suited to the same type of grazing as sheep. If your grazing is quite long and rich, you must cut down your pony's time at grass, but only an expert on the spot, such as your instructor, the yard owner or your vet, can advise you on this. Whomever you get to advise you on land care, do stress that the land is for ponies and must not produce rich grass, as for cattle. There are special seed mixes that will produce the right kind of grass, if reseeding is needed, but your expert or consultant will advise you on this. Sometimes the land can be strip-grazed with electric fencing, or divided into smaller areas to cut down the amount of grass available to the pony, and, again, your consultant can advise you.

FENCES

The fencing and gates in the field are also important. They must keep the pony in without putting him in danger. Barbed wire is a very common fencing material, particularly on fields rented from farmers, but it can be very dangerous for ponies. They can be seriously cut and injured on it. They gallop and play about more than cattle, and can easily end up in the fencing, with disastrous results. Post and rail fencing is the best, or posts with smooth, plain wire, or, of course, thick natural hedges. Any fencing should be at least the height of the pony's back and preferably higher.

GATES

Gates should be strong and either of wood or smooth metal, preferably with the bottom half filled in with a strong metal grille to prevent the ponies getting their legs caught in the lower bars. The gate should be fastened with a smooth bolt, not a hunting latch which sticks up and is meant to be operated from horseback, or a spring clip or hook of some kind, as these can all be dangerous and

injure the ponies if they start playing about with them. All wood should be treated with preservative to help delay rotting, but not creosote, which can be poisonous if ponies lick or chew the wood.

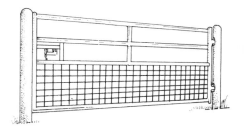

A safe, strong metal gate with the bottom half filled in with strong metal mesh (not just wire netting) so the ponies cannot get their feet through the bars. The bolt is set under a bar so it is more difficult for the ponies to interfere with it and undo the gate.

SHELTER

If there is no real shelter, such as lots of high, thick hedges and trees, there should be a shelter shed in the field. It should be positioned on the highest part of the field so that the ground inside doesn't become boggy with rainwater, and its back should face the direction from which the wind usually comes in your area. Look on a still day to see if the trees are bent, as if growing in one direction: if so, they will bend *away* from the prevailing wind, so the open front of your shed should face the way the trees seem to bend.

WATER

The field will need a water supply and it's best not to rely on streams or ponds, which can have dangerous

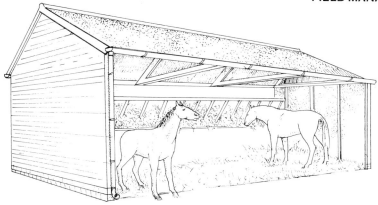

Shelter is very important to ponies out for more than a few hours a day. This one is ideal being roomy with a high entrance and open front, encouraging the animals to enter. It is bedded down comfortably and has a supply of hay in the rack along the back wall so they don't go hungry when grass is scarce. The guttering and a drain pipe ensures that water doesn't fall down from the front edge and put the ponies off going in or out.

approaches and be polluted without looking as though they are. In fact, it's often best to fence off ponds as ponies can get stuck in them; if they are at all deep and freeze over in winter, ponies can fall through the ice if they try to walk on it, and drown. Ditches and dykes should really be fenced off for the same reason. Ponies also often roll near them and if they fall into the ditch and get stuck they can die from drowning, cold or the exhaustion of struggling to get out.

The most convenient type of water supply for a field is to pipe it to the field from the mains, to a trough with an automatic filling device of some sort (either a pressure fill or a ballcock device). All troughs should be sited on a high part of the field as ponies' hooves can soon make the surrounding area very muddy, which can put off some sensitive ponies from drinking. There should be no sharp edges or corners on the trough and the filling device should be covered to protect it from the ponies interfering with it.

If piped water is not laid on, you can rig up a dustbin rammed into a lorry or tractor tyre (see picture) and tied to the fence, filled from a nearby tap by hosepipe. If this is not possible either, water will have to be transported to the field in a water bowser (a container on wheels) and left for the ponies, being replaced by a full one probably every day, and twice a day in hot weather. A pony can drink up to about 36 litres (roughly 8 gal) of water daily in hot weather, so a large amount will be needed, depending on the number of ponies in the field.

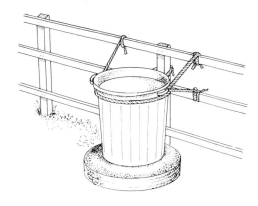

CHAPTER 10

HEALTH AND SICKNESS

No matter how well you look after your pony, there will be times when he is injured or ill. Ponies are active and work for their living, and knocks, cuts and strained muscles and joints are fairly common. With good management, actual diseases should be less common although most ponies will be ill at some time in their lives.

SIGNS OF GOOD HEALTH

You need to know what a really healthy pony looks like before you can tell if your pony is a bit off colour, or actually ill.

A healthy pony will have a smooth, glossy, fairly shiny coat even if he lives at grass and gets muddy. The underlying sheen to his coat and the lively, smooth feel to the hair will still be obvious. If his coat feels hard and stiff, looks dull or is standing up away from his skin (called 'staring') he could be ill. Don't confuse this with the woolly coat of winter which may look staring but which is still glossy and has a lively feel. The pony's skin should be easily

A sick pony will look very 'hang-dog' and miserable and may stand like this, head down and still, away from other ponies or at the back of his stable.

moved over his ribs: put the flat of your hand on his side and see how easily you can move the skin around. If you don't get much movement and the skin feels as though it is stuck to his ribs this could be a sign of trouble; it is called being 'hidebound'.

Other signs of possible sickness are dull eyes; they may even appear sunk in their sockets. He will be dull and lacking in energy and feel more sluggish than usual to ride or handle. He may keep away from other ponies (who may also pick on him, recognizing his weakness), and may stand with his head down looking miserable for quite long periods. He may lie down a lot for more than half an hour at a time, may not want his food, and generally not look or behave like his usual self. If you have even a small feeling that something is not right with your pony, do tell someone experienced as delay could make any illness harder to treat.

WHAT SORT OF THING CAN GO WRONG?

Lameness caused by an injured or diseased foot or leg is quite common in many horses and ponies, particularly those kept in dangerous conditions where they can injure themselves easily, treading on rough ground when moving fast, getting caught in fencing, and so on, or those working hard where knocks and strains are likely. It's sometimes difficult to spot lameness, but if it is at all serious the pony will limp. Your yard owner or instructor will confirm whether or not the pony is lame, and may or may not call the vet, depending on what the cause might be.

Laminitis is a disease of the foot which definitely causes lameness, but as ponies usually get it in both of a pair of feet (say both front or both hind) the limping may not be so noticeable as both feet are painful. The pony will

This pony has laminitis, a very painful foot disease, and is standing with his weight back on his heels to take the weight off the most painful part of his feet, at the front.

Wounds are of several types and can be caused by tearing on wire, bruises which also damage the skin, punctures and straightforward cuts. Do not delay treating a wound, particularly in getting it clean and stopping bleeding, as delay can allow infection, which will make healing more difficult. Some wounds may need stitching, some may need bandaging and others may be so slight they can be left uncovered. Always get expert help with wounds, although it is not always necessary to call the vet.

A nasty wound on a pony's back which could have been caused by a badly fitting saddle or because the pony rolled on a sharp stone in the field. This will take a long time to heal and the pony will be out of work until it does.

not want to move much, and may stand leaning backwards to take the weight off his front feet; or, if the hind feet are affected, with his hind feet well under his body. Laminitis is caused by over-feeding, giving too-rich food or by some blood disorder. It is also caused by allowing the feet to grow too long at the toe, and by jarring through riding the pony too fast on hard ground (including roads or frozen or baked fields).

The sensitive and insensitive laminae, which are joined together in the feet, come apart, sometimes so badly that the pedal bone starts to move downwards, actually pressing on or even through the sole of the foot. Laminitis is an extremely painful disease and you must call your vet in at once to treat it and advise on future feeding and care.

Colic is a form of indigestion. For some reason the food is not being digested properly in the stomach or intestines and the pony is in pain. Because ponies have long intestines and delicate digestions, veterinary attention is always needed quickly with colic. Your pony will look miserable and uncomfortable and, if the pain in his belly is bad, he may look frightened. He may sweat in patches, may look round anxiously at his sides, maybe biting at them, may be restless, may groan with pain and may try to roll a lot. Whatever time of day or night it is, weekday or weekend, you must call the vet at once for colic, and get instructions on the telephone as to what to do until he or she arrives.

Equine influenza, or 'flu, is serious in ponies and can cause weakened lungs for the rest of the pony's life, particularly if he is not allowed a long enough recovery time afterwards. Your pony will look unhappy, and will have no energy or interest in anything. He will probably have a high temperature (ask your yard owner or someone experienced to take it for you) and a watery discharge from his nose. He may feel hot, but shiver, and may or may not cough. Get him into a well-ventilated loose box, and put on a rug or two to keep him warm, and call the vet at once.

Coughing has many causes and some coughs are no more than a pony clearing his throat. However, coughing can indicate that he has a disease or allergy, often to stable dust. If your pony coughs, which sounds like a short barking noise with the head down, or a softer, deeper noise, tell your yard owner or someone else experienced at once and keep a close eye on him for further coughs. If it carries on for a day, call the vet at once.

Strangles is another serious lung and throat disease, mostly caught by youngish ponies. It can cause permanent lung and heart damage. Sometimes it follows the 'flu. Again, the pony will feel and look ill and his throat may feel and look swollen, hard and lumpy, which means that his glands are swollen. Get him into an airy loose box, keep him well rugged up, and call the vet at once.

PREVENTING ILLNESS

Consult with your vet about what vaccinations your pony should have, and when. He or she will certainly recommend vaccinations against 'flu and a disease called tetanus or lockjaw (caused by a germ which can enter through the tiniest wound and which can kill your pony). Advice will also be given on checking the pony's teeth, as they can develop sharp edges and corners which cut the inside of the mouth. He will also advise on when to give the pony worming medicines to kill worms inside the pony. Most

ponies have worms but if you keep the levels very low with regular medicines they do little damage. Good land management helps keep down worm infestation, but worming all the ponies in the yard at the same time is an important part of correct care. Lungworms, which are a cause of coughing and faulty breathing, can also be caught and treated.

Your vet is a valuable friend when it comes to getting correct advice, not

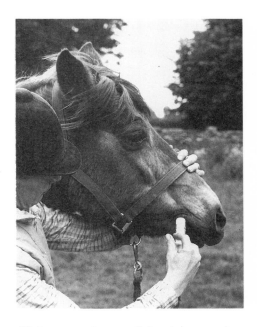

Giving worming medicine to a pony is easy. Your vet will supply the medicine in a plastic syringe like this. You put it in the corner of the mouth, pointing it towards the back of the throat, then press the plunger down and the paste medicine will be squirted to the back of the throat and the pony will – we hope – swallow it. If you only get the medicine into his mouth near the front, he will spit it out. Steady his head with your free hand, like this.

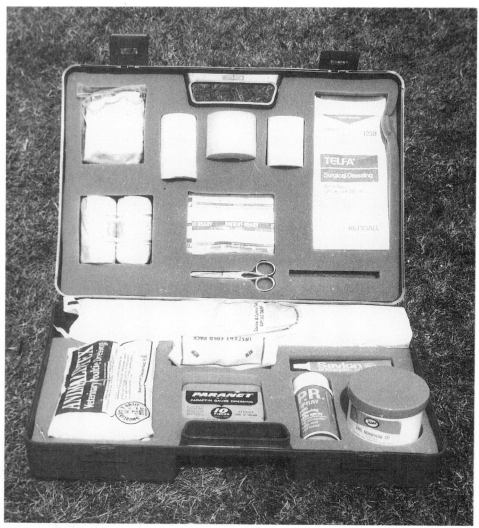

A useful first aid kit for travelling or keeping in the tack room. You can buy them from good saddlers, by mail order from horse magazines, or through your vet.

only on treating your pony when he is ill but also on keeping him healthy in the first place, so do ask for his help on anything you are unsure of.

You can learn about illnesses and what you yourself can do to keep the pony healthy and how to treat simple disorders (called 'first aid') by reading a good, up-to-date book on the subject, such as *Horse Health Care* by Janet Eley, published by Ward Lock. Keep such a book handy for when you need it – but read it first to learn all you can about veterinary subjects. Don't be alarmed at all the things that can go wrong with your pony. With good care and help from your vet you should not have too much trouble.

CHAPTER 11

TRAVELLING

Most ponies have to travel at some time in their lives, and a lot of them are quite frightened of it. A few cannot be travelled at all, and this obviously cuts down what you can do with them – no travelling to shows or riding centres for lessons, and so on. Ponies may become difficult to travel because they have been badly treated in the past when travelling. Once they have become difficult to travel it is hard to improve them as they have very long memories and will be frightened of the same bad experiences being repeated.

Walk confidently up the ramp, really believing your pony will go in the box, and he probably will! Enjoy your day out!

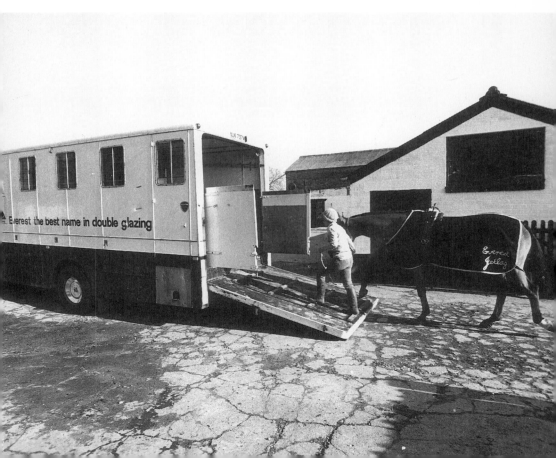

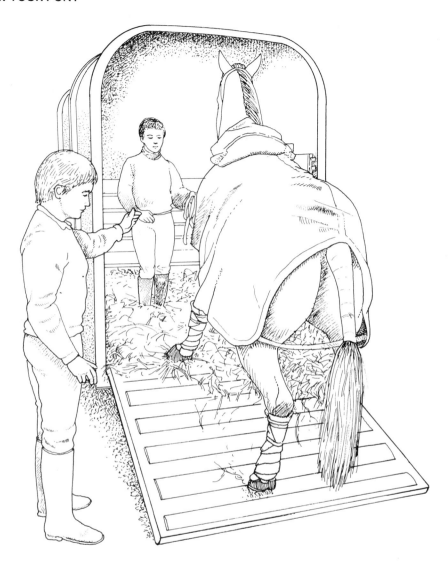

A big disadvantage with many trailers is that you have to back the pony down to get him out. Most ponies find this difficult and are frightened of doing it. Someone should stand ready to guide him down the ramp and reassure him. Don't rush him.

DIFFERENT VEHICLES

You can travel a pony in a trailer towed behind a car, or a proper horsebox. Horseboxes are by far the best as they are roomier, safer and give a steadier feel, but they can be more expensive. You can get small horseboxes suitable for carrying one or two horses or ponies, and they can work out very economical to run. The extra convenience, comfort and safety they offer make them very much worthwhile.

Many people get together and hire a box and driver for shows or hunting, and this is cheaper if you do not have enough journeys planned to make it worthwhile getting your own vehicle. Unfortunately, some cheap transporters only have cattle wagons to hire and these are neither suitable nor safe for horses and ponies, despite being used a lot. Horseboxes and trailers have proper partitions to separate the animals where more than one is being travelled, but cattle wagons only have single poles across the wagon to separate them. This can result in ponies perhaps falling and being trampled on by others, or being trodden on or kicked whether they fall or not, and being bitten. No matter how badly you want to go to a particular event, don't travel your pony in a cattle wagon.

In any vehicle, your pony should have at least 30 cm (1 ft) on each side of him and in front of and behind his breast and tail. He must not be cramped up as he could be frightened, and will also be very stiff on arrival. He will be tied up in the vehicle but the rope needs to be long enough to let him stand straight and move his head from side to side, but not so long that he can turn it right round or so that it loops down and he can get a leg over it. Most trailers do not allow nearly enough headroom, because if they are high enough to allow the preferred 1 m (3 ft 3 in) above the head height of the pony, they will cause wind resistance behind the car, which can cause dangerous swaying. (Another excellent reason for investing in a small horsebox.) Your parents, or whoever owns the trailer or box, will be responsible for maintaining it and keeping it in good, safe condition. The floor, in particular, should be kept very strong, as should the ramp up which the pony will enter the vehicle. There should not be a wide gap between the ramp and the floor of the vehicle as ponies can get their legs down here with disastrous results.

All vehicles should be properly maintained, and have good ventilation, as stuffy air can cause disease and make the pony feel travel sick. As ponies cannot vomit, they have no way of relieving this terrible feeling and become very ill. It can even cause colic. They also need a secure feeling beneath their feet, and various non-slip mats are available for flooring boxes and trailers. In addition, a good, thick bed of straw or damp sawdust is an excellent idea and will certainly make the pony feel safer and give him a secure foothold. Spread bedding on the ramp, too, to make loading and unloading less worrying for him.

Some ponies are difficult to load and unload, and, in any case, as a novice you will leave this job to someone experienced. If your pony causes trouble, however, remember it is usually because he is frightened, not because he is stroppy, and it is absolutely pointless, and the worst possible horsemastership, to thrash him. No matter who they are, never let anyone thrash your pony if he is reluctant to go into his vehicle. Get more expert help if you are having problems. Kindness, firmness and confidence are the keys to persuading ponies to enter and leave the vehicle, and there are various methods to encourage difficult ponies that will not make them worse.

THE DRIVER

The driver also makes a big difference to how well a pony travels. He or she should speed up, change gear and slow down very smoothly and gradually indeed, as any change in speed and direction upsets the pony's balance – and remember, he cannot prepare for this by altering his position as he cannot see or sense what is going on. Sudden jerks backwards, forwards or sideways are very frightening for him. The driver should also corner, go round roundabouts and change lanes on main roads or motorways very gradually and smoothly, and generally take things slowly when doing anything which takes the vehicle away from a constant speed and a straight line.

If your pony panics during the journey you must stop, especially if you are towing a trailer, as the trailer might overturn and cause a terrible accident, or the pony might seriously injure himself. You cannot, by law, travel in the back of a trailer, but if you feel the car lurching around or see it swaying, or see the pony, through the little window at the front if there is one, playing up, do stop and go to him to calm him down, but stay outside his compartment. In a horsebox you may travel in the back if you wish, and can go into the back during the journey (if you can get straight through from the cab) should the pony be upset. However, panic-stricken ponies can be very dangerous, so you are best to leave this to someone experienced.

The best advice for anyone driving a horse or pony in either a trailer or a horsebox is: drive as though you had no brakes.

INDEX

Page numbers in *italic* refer to illustrations